SOUTHERN CALIFORNIA TRIVIA

Seana Graham & Lisa Wojna

Illustrations by Peter Tyler & Roger Garcia

BLUE
BIKE
BOOKS

The Publisher: Blue Bike Books

Library and Archives Canada Cataloguing in Publication

Graham, Seana, 1956–
        Bathroom book of Southern California trivia : weird, wacky and wild / Seana Graham and Lisa Wojna.

ISBN-13: 978-1-897278-29-1
ISBN-10: 1-897278-29-2

        1. California, Southern—Miscellanea. I. Wojna, Lisa, 1962– II. Title.
F867.G76 2007   979.4'9   C2007-901522-0

Project Director: Nicholle Carrière
Project Editor: Sheila Quinlan
Cover Image: Roger Garcia
Illustrations: Peter Tyler, Roger Garcia and Patrick Hénaff

We acknowledge the support of the Alberta Foundation for the Arts for our publishing program.

Alberta Foundation for the Arts

PC: 5

DEDICATION

For Rupert Francis Enever, 1958–2006

I'm not quite sure what you'd make of having a trivia book dedicated to you, Rupert, but I hope you'd be amused.

—Seana

ACKNOWLEDGMENTS

Thanks to Nicholle Carrière for giving me the opportunity to try this project and for her gentle encouragement along the way, and to Sheila Quinlan for her close reading and constructive comments, which have made this a much better book than it would have been. My family and friends, too numerous to mention, have helped me keep faith in the writing life time and again. Thanks to all for the many kinds of support shown through this sometimes daunting project. You know who you are.

—Seana

Many thanks to my clever editor Sheila, who pieced together the work of two authors and did so seamlessly; and to my family— my husband Garry, sons Peter, Matthew and Nathan, daughter Melissa and granddaughter Jada. Without you, all this and anything else I do in my life would be meaningless.

—Lisa

CONTENTS

SPORTS

MISCELLANEOUS

INTRODUCTION

I can't say that I grew up thinking of myself as a trivia writer in the making. But looking back, there were telltale signs. Not long after I learned to read, my parents invested in the *World Book Encyclopedia*, and I soon became fixated on the idea of reading from the beginning of the "A"s right through to the end of the "Z"s. Plus the yearly supplements. Not that I actually did this, of course—that would have revealed a different sort of vocation, maybe to be a prize-winning quiz show contestant or a Rhodes Scholar. No, the way I perused the encyclopedia was to dabble in it, picking up facts here and there as one picks up pretty pebbles in a stream. Admittedly, my attention was more likely to be riveted by a complete set of color plates of various dog breeds than the properties of uranium, but I'm sure I also picked up a little of the more esoteric sort of knowledge in this haphazard way.

Joseph Campbell famously advised "follow your bliss," and it seems that Southern Californians have never needed much persuading to do just that. Whether tunneling straight through a mountain for reasons known only to oneself, or staging a weekly dance performance in a renovated Death Valley theater even if no one shows up to watch, Southern Californians don't seem to spend a lot of time worrying about what the neighbors will think. I'm particularly impressed with the many highly individual women we've come across in the course of researching this book, such as artist Beatrice Wood and dancer Marta Becket, who found their true vocations in California.

Although it would have been encouraging if I'd read it earlier, it was actually towards the end of this project that I came by chance upon a quote from William Van Horne: "Nothing is too small to know and nothing too big to attempt." While there were definitely times when I wasn't sure of the truth of the last part of that statement when it came to tackling a subject as vast as Southern California, I have only become more convinced of

the first part. So many of these small pieces of seemingly incon-
sequential knowledge are in fact tied in strange and sometimes
even moving ways to much bigger stories. Little did I know, for
instance, that a somewhat random fact gleaned about camels
wandering around the Hollywood Hills in the late 1800s would
lead to learning about an interesting experiment of the United
States Army, and that those camels' fates were very much tied to
the United States Civil War. Curious? Read on.

I wonder if my fellow trivia writers in this series would agree
that there is a sort of Peter's Principle involved when it comes to
gathering trivia—namely, that the best piece of trivia you will
ever discover is pretty much guaranteed to be the one you'll
come across the day after you turn in the manuscript. But
there's a hidden consolation in this possibility. It means that
there are still a lot more fun, quirky, interesting facts about
Southern California out there to discover. I invite you, dear
reader, to join in the hunt.

WHAT SETS SOUTHERN CALIFORNIA APART

California Dreaming

Maybe there's something about the light. It turns out that something special really does happen when airborne dust meets marine air—the dust becomes reflective, creating a sort of perpetual white haze. And no, that's not just the smog.

California was a land of myths and dreams long before the advent of motion pictures—film was just a bonus. You could say it started with the Spaniards and their dream of New Spain, but why pick just them? There have been railroad dreamers and orange-grove dreamers, canal-building dreamers and dreamers of riches who were sure they'd strike gold in the next stream or black gold if only they drilled an oil well in their backyard. Mystic dreamers have founded their own sects in some California canyons, some of those sects not so benign. Of course there were the moviemakers, who would end up projecting their dreams on screens around the world. And we haven't even gotten to Walt Disney yet, who just may have been the biggest dreamer of them all.

The automobile brought new dreams. The city of Los Angeles is the only major city in the world that has been planned around the car and probably one of the few that actually sits atop a convenient basin of oil. Fill 'er up!

Stupendous Southern California

It's the beach and the glam and the glitz that the world sees, but Southern California is really a kind of perpetually pulsing machine beneath that deceptive surface. It's got some of the most cutting-edge research facilities in the world for nanotechnology and biomedicine and who knows just what else—what's important is that the region has money and power and the savvy to use them. In just a few hundred years, Southern California has been through all kinds of booms and busts, and it will probably go through a few more. But it's pretty sure to pick itself up, dust itself off and start off in some new direction no one could have predicted.

And if all else fails, there's always the beach.

WHAT'S IN A NAME?

A Legendary Land

If the meaning behind a name bears any responsibility for the personality of a place, it's no wonder California is a mysterious land where almost anything goes and imagination rules. *Las Sergas de Esplandian* was a wild romance written by Garcia Montalvo in 1510. The story told of an island named California that abounded in pearls and gold and was inhabited solely by a race of Amazonian black women. Men were welcomed to its shores but once a year and for one purpose only—to procreate. Any man attempting access to its shores at any other time was killed and fed to the griffins.

In any case, early explorers discovering pearls in modern day California thought they'd discovered the mythical land of Montalvo's story. And despite the somewhat tumultuous development of the state, during which many nations attempted to lay claim to the land, the name stuck.

DID YOU  KNOW?

The ownership of California was obviously a contentious issue. Russia, Spain, Mexico and the United States all erected flags on California soil, each laying claim to the state at different points in its early history.

MAKING IT OFFICIAL

Welcome to the Union

California received its admission to statehood on September 9, 1850, making it the 31st state of the United States of America.

Flying High

California's original state flag was first raised on June 14, 1846—four years before the region received statehood status. The flag was painted by William Todd as a visible statement that the American settlers of the Sonoma area weren't happy with the Mexican government of the day. The original flag, consisting of a grizzly bear, a five-pointed red star and the words "California Republic," painted on little more than a scrap of brown cotton, was raised in Sonoma on June 14, 1846, in a protest known as the Bear Flag Revolt. Sadly, the original flag was destroyed in the Great Earthquake and Fire of 1906. The modern version of this original flag was officially adopted in 1911.

What's Wrong with This Picture?

Given its prominence on the state flag, it's no surprise that California's state animal is the California grizzly bear (*Ursus californicus*). It earned this honor in 1953, sadly, a full 31 years after the last of this largest and most powerful native carnivore roaming the lowlands of the state was killed.

DID YOU KNOW?

The last California grizzly was hunted down and killed in Tulare County in August 1922.

Literally translated, California's state motto *Eureka* means "I have found it." It is thought that the term initially referred to the discovery of gold in California. The motto was officially adopted in 1963, despite earlier attempts to adopt the more traditional "In God We Trust."

Golden in So Many Ways

California's nickname is the "Golden State." The moniker was made official in 1968, and though some people think it refers to the Gold Rush of California's early history, it's actually in reference to the California hillsides, which typically turn golden brown during the summer months.

Official Offerings

☛ The Great Seal—a picturesque snapshot of California with the Roman goddess Minerva featured prominently, along with 31 stars representing the states of the Union—was officially adopted during the Constitutional Convention of 1849. Of course, California didn't officially become a state until the following year, but that didn't seem like anything more than a minor inconvenience.

☛ The golden poppy (*Eschscholtzia californica*), which grows wild throughout the state, was named California's official flower in 1903. It's so popular that in 1974, the legislature designated April 6 as California Poppy Day.

☛ The California valley quail (*Lophortyx californica*) was adopted as the state bird in 1931.

☛ Among California's first official symbols is the Pasadena Playhouse. It earned the honor as the official state theater in 1937.

☞ California's native redwood was named the state's official tree in 1937, but this initial designation didn't mention a specific species of redwood. California has two species that are considered native to the state—the coast redwood (*Sequoia sempervirens*) and the giant sequoia (*Sequoiadendron giganteum*)—so both were given the honor in the amended declaration of 1953.

☞ The California golden trout (*Salmo augua-bonita*) was named the state's official fish in 1947.

☞ Blue and gold were adopted as the official state colors in 1951. The color blue represents the sky, and gold represents the color of the precious metal that initiated a flood of miners to the area in the early days of the state's history.

☞ "I Love You, California," penned by F.B. Silverwood, put to music by A.F. Frankenstein and first published in 1913, was named the state's official song in 1951.

☞ Because gold fever was at least partially responsible for the population explosion that California experienced in the years following gold's discovery in 1848, it makes sense that gold is the state's official mineral. It was so named in 1965.

☞ Serpentine was named California's official rock in 1965.

☞ Unique to the foothills of the Sierra Nevadas and coastal areas from Sonoma to San Diego, the California dogface butterfly (*Zerene eurydice*) was named the state's official insect in 1972.

☞ The desert tortoise (*Gopherus agassizii*) was named California's official state reptile in 1972. It is now an endangered species.

☞ The long-toothed, ferocious meat-eater known as the saber-toothed cat (*Smilodon californicus*) was named the state's official fossil in 1973. The feline, which lived about 11,000 years ago, earned this honor because abundant skeletal remains of the cat have been discovered in the tar pits of Rancho La Brea in Los Angeles.

☛ The California gray whale (*Eschrichtius robustus*), which measures up to 50 feet in length and weighs in anywhere from 20 to 40 tons, was named California's official marine mammal in 1975.

☛ In 1979, the state legislature designated the California Historical Society its official historical society.

☛ The blue diamond—as rare and precious as it is expensive—was named California's state gemstone in 1985. The blue beauty, also known as benitoite, was first discovered in California in the San Benito River.

☛ Although its roots can be traced back to the swing, whip or jitterbug dances of the 1930s, West Coast Swing is a 100-percent pure California product. It's no wonder, then, that it was named the state's official dance in 1988. The state's official folk dance—none other than the square dance—was also declared that same year.

☛ California was the first state to designate an official prehistoric artifact. What appears to be a miniature bear carved from volcanic rock was uncovered from a dig in San Diego County in 1985. Measuring 2.5 by 1.5 inches, the Chipped Stone Bear was named the state's official prehistoric artifact in 1991.

☛ Patriotic to the core, California adopted the California Consolidated Drum Band as its official fife and drum band in 1997.

☛ San Joaquin soil was named California's official state soil in 1997, but really, who knew soil could be so interesting? According to some sources, San Joaquin soil could be up to

250,000 years old and was one of the original soils studied in the state. The 1997 designation coincided with the completion of the state's most comprehensive soil inventory to date.

☛ The blue, green, red and gold of the John Muir family tartan was the basis for California's official tartan. Officially adopted in 2001, the tartan was chosen in honor of Muir, the state's well-loved naturalist, explorer and conservationist. Incidentally, a year later the state legislature also declared April 6 to be California Tartan Day—apparently poppies and tartan go together.

☛ It's no wonder that California has a designated official Gold Rush ghost town. Earning the title in 2002, the town of Bodie had a population of about 10,000 in its boom years. Located northeast of Yosemite and south of Bridgeport, the town stands as a visual reminder of a bygone era and was officially named a National Historic Site and a California State Historic Park in 1962.

☛ California has an official state military museum, and it is none other than the California State Military Museum and Resource Center, located in the Old Sacramento State Historic Park. It received its official designation in 2004.

☛ Purple needlegrass (*Nassella pulchra*) was named California's official grass in 2004.

MORE THAN JUST SUNSHINE

Rainfall

The rainy season in Southern California extends from November to March, with the heaviest showers typically occurring from December through February. Because most winter storms come in from the north, rainfall tends to diminish as you go farther south. So average rainfall in Santa Barbara is about 17 inches per year, Los Angeles gets around 15 inches, and San Diego gets an average of 10 inches per year. Imperial County, in the southeastern part of the state, records about three inches each year, while a true desert area such as Death Valley can expect only 1.7 inches of annual rainfall.

Thunderstorms

Thunderstorms can occur year-round throughout California. Areas of higher elevation, such as the Sierra Nevadas, can see thunderstorms of varying severity between 50 and 60 times each year.

Tornadoes

California, on average, experiences only about six tornadoes per year, based on statistics gathered from 1951 to 2000. Most twisters occur in the Central Valley and Los Angeles Basin.

Snowfall

Almost every part of California has experienced snowfall, though it is most common in mountain areas. Snow has even fallen in Death Valley, an arid desert.

Average Growing Season

The southernmost portion of the California coast usually boasts a growing season that is 365 days long. The average growing season in the Sierra Nevadas, however, is only 50 days.

Walls of Water

Surfs crest along the California coastline throughout the year, but in spring, they measure about five feet or so—a perfect crest for the avid surfer. However, since the average water temperature along the San Francisco coastline is in the 50°F range, folks tend to prefer California's more southern beaches. Water temperatures there average about 10 degrees warmer.

AVERAGES AND EXTREMES

Palmdale (the High Desert)

Average summer high is 98°F, and average winter high is 59°F.
Average summer low is 65°F, and average winter low is 33°F.

Holtville (the Southern Border)

Average summer high is 107°F, and average winter high is 54°F.
Average summer low is 58°F, and average winter low is 42°F.

Santa Monica (the Coast)

Average summer high is 70°F, and average winter high is 65°F.
Average summer low is 55°F, and average winter low is 50°F.

Lake Arrowhead (the Mountains)

Average summer high is 97°F, and average winter high is 61°F.
Average summer low is 57°F, and average winter low is 37°F.

Beverly Hills (Just Because)

Average summer high is 92°F, and average winter high is 67°F.
Average summer low is 74°F, and average winter low is 46°F.

CLASSIC CALIFORNIA

Death Valley earns top spot as the hottest place on Earth. From July 6 to August 17, 1917, the area recorded 43 consecutive days of 120-plus degrees Fahrenheit temperatures.

Weather Extremes

California routinely experiences extended periods of drought, some as long as 80 years in duration. One source points to the year 1625 as California's driest in history. Here are a few California extremes from the 20th century:

☞ Highest recorded temperature: 134°F, Death Valley, July 10, 1913

☞ Lowest recorded temperature: −45°F, Boca, January 20, 1937

- Largest amount of rainfall in one hour: 4.7 inches, Mt. Palomar, August 13, 1992

- Largest amount of rainfall in 24 hours: 26.12 inches, Hoegees Camp, January 22, 1943

- Largest amount of rainfall in one month: 81.9 inches, Camp 6, December 1981

- Largest amount of rainfall in one season: 257.9 inches, Camp 6, 1982

- Smallest amount of rainfall in one season: 0 inches, Death Valley, 1929

- Largest amount of snowfall in 24 hours: 67 inches, Echo Summit, January 4–5, 1982

- Largest amount of snowfall in one storm: 189 inches, Shasta Ski Bowl, February 13–19, 1959

- Largest amount of snowfall in one month: 390 inches, Tamarack, January 1911

- Largest amount of snowfall in one season: 884 inches, Tamarack, 1906–07

- Deepest snow cover: 451 inches, Tamarack, March 11, 1911

- Highest wind velocity: 101 miles per hour, Sandberg, March 25, 1975

TOP 10 WEATHER DISASTERS OF THE LAST 100 YEARS

1. More than They Bargained For
In January 1915, the San Diego City Council approached a famous rainmaker named Charles Hatfield to provide enough rain to fill the Morena Dam Reservoir. The council eventually agreed to give him $10,000, payable when the reservoir was full. He set up operations near Lake Morena early in 1916. On January 5, the rain came, and it proceeded to grow heavier every day—until it had washed out most of San Diego's bridges, overflowed two dams and, finally, caused the Lower Otay Dam to burst on January 27. At least a dozen people were killed, and some estimates claim closer to 30 people died in the disaster. Although Hatfield said the damage was not his fault and that he had fulfilled his side of the bargain, the city refused to pay him unless he also took on the liability for the flood damage, which was already being estimated at $3.5 million. Hatfield tried to sue the council and went to court twice, but in both cases the rain was declared an Act of God—in other words, not an act of Hatfield's.

2. A Bit of Overcompensation?
The Los Angeles flood of 1938 began on February 27 after three days of heavy rain, when the Los Angeles River overflowed its banks, killing 115 people and destroying 5601 homes. As a result, new flood control measures were enacted, and the Army Corps of Engineers encased the river's bed and banks in concrete. Today, there are very few parts of the river that aren't completely wrapped in concrete.

3. We Don't Get Hurricanes in California—Do We?
Well, maybe not, but on September 25, 1939, a tropical storm of near-hurricane proportions made landfall at Long Beach, the

only tropical storm to do so in known history. Torrential rains dumped almost six inches of precipitation in just 24 hours, and 45 deaths were reported on land alone.

4. Bel Air Blazes
Dry land and strong winds led to the Bel Air fire of 1961. Not only did firefighters have to contend with dangerous conditions and rapidly spreading flames, but poor urban planning left them without adequate street access. Families fled their homes with little more than the clothes on their backs and the few possessions they could carry. Over 100 firefighters were injured, and the total cost of this disaster was $100 million from the loss of 484 buildings and damage to more than 6000 acres.

DID YOU  KNOW?

As in so many of Southern California's disasters, celebrities took their hits in the Bel Air fire just as much as the common folk did. Burt Lancaster, Joan Bennett and Zsa Zsa Gabor had homes that were burned to the ground in the conflagration. And the names of those whose houses barely escaped total destruction reads like a stroll down the Walk of Fame: Cary Grant, Red Skelton, Kim Novak, Alfred Hitchcock, Ginger Rogers and Marlon Brando are but a few stars whose homes were damaged or threatened in the fire.

5. Dust in the Wind
Winds gusting 192 miles per hour in Arvin in Kern County quite literally changed the landscape in December 1977. More than 25 million tons of soil drifted away, and fertile farmland was transformed into sandy soil, causing the agriculture industry in the area to suffer for many years afterwards. Three people died, and there were $40 million in immediate economic losses.

6. Great Balls of Fire

What started out as 20 separate fires combined and were propelled by dry, windy weather throughout Southern California
in October 1993. The resulting devastation included four dead,
162 injured, 194,000 acres damaged and $1 billion in economic
losses.

7. Cold Snap

Although exact damages aren't available, Southern California's
orange, lemon and other citrus fruit crops suffered, in some cases,
irreparable damage when temperatures dipped between 10°F and
15°F for several days in January 1913. The extreme weather led to
the development of the fruit frost forecast program.

8. Dry Years...

There's no doubt, moderation is key when it comes to precipitation. While excessive moisture has caused no end of problems
throughout history, drought has been just as damaging. Drought
conditions in California from 1975 to 1977 resulted in disaster
declarations in 31 counties and $2.6 billion in economic losses.
And a six-year drought as recently as 1987–92 created an unprec-
edented statewide water emergency.

9. And Wet Ones

Excessive precipitation, damaging winds, mudslides and overflow-
ing rivers across most of the state—all were the result of El Niño
storms in 1982 and 1983. Forty-six of California's 58 counties
were declared disaster areas. At least 36 people were killed, 481
injured, and 6661 homes and 1330 businesses were damaged or
destroyed.

10. Cross-Country Conflagration

President George W. Bush declared San Bernardino, San Diego,
Ventura and Los Angeles counties all to be major disaster areas in
October 2003 after deadly fires, fueled at least in part by Santa
Ana winds, scorched more than 300,000 acres as far north as the

Simi Valley and all the way south to San Diego County. More than 8000 firefighters were called in to try to contain at least 10 separate fires.

DID YOU KNOW?

One of the fires that caused the most loss of life and property damage was the Cedar Fire, which killed 14 civilians and one firefighter and injured 113 additional firefighters. It was caused by a deer hunter named Sergio Martinez, who had become separated from his hunting partner and was lost for over 11 hours. He had learned in a safety class that one should set a fire as a last resort when lost, which he did—with catastrophic consequences. Although the judge gave him a light sentence because he hadn't set the fire with reckless intent, a few people felt differently about it, and one woman put a cheap whistle she had bought at Wal-Mart on the defense table where he sat, suggesting that he use *that* if he ever got lost in the woods again.

11. (One More for Good Measure)
January 7 through January 11, 2005, saw an almost unabated period of heavy rain in Southern California, with the hardest hit areas being from Point Conception west of Santa Barbara and inland towards the San Gabriel and San Bernardino mountains lying north and east of L.A. Loss of life included 10 people killed in mudslides in the small coastal community of La Conchita in Ventura County. At its peak, the storm was dropping two inches of rain every six hours for roughly 36 hours, the greatest amount being 4.37 inches at Nordhoff Ridge near Ojai around 4:00AM on January 9. Although all Southern California river basins felt the effects of this massive precipitation, the highest flows were recorded for the Ventura River and the Santa Clara River north-west of Los Angeles.

A GENEROUS GEOGRAPHY

Regional Divides

Arid deserts, lush green valleys, majestic mountains and coast-line as far as the eye can see—when it comes to variety of land-scape and natural features, California has it all. Generally speaking, the geography of California can be divided into eight main regions:

☞ the Klamath Mountains in the northwest;

☞ the Coastal Ranges, which extend the length of the state;

☞ the Sierra Nevadas, which cover almost the entire eastern region;

☞ the Central Valley, which extends for almost 400 miles down the middle of the state;

☞ the Cascade Mountains, which start in British Columbia and extend down to the northern part of California;

☞ the Basin and Range Region, which includes the south-eastern desert areas of California;

☞ the Los Angeles Ranges, which are a group of small mountain regions between Santa Barbara and San Diego counties in the south;

☞ and the San Diego Ranges, which cover much of the far south western part of the state.

TRIVIAL NUMEROLOGICAL GEOGRAPHICAL DATA

Location, Location, Location

The 770-mile-long and 250-mile-wide state of California is located on the country's Pacific coast, bordered by Oregon to the north, Nevada and Arizona to the east and Mexico to the south.

Overall Size

California is the third largest state, covering an area of 163,707 square miles. Still, it seriously lags behind Texas, which is in second place with 268,601 square miles, and first place Alaska with 656,424 square miles.

Surf and Turf

Of its total area, 155,973 square miles are land and 7734 square miles are water. Forests cover about 35 percent of California's landmass, while deserts take up about 25 percent.

That's a Lot of Oceanfront Property

While the state measures only 770 miles from north to south, its coastline covers 840 miles. This distance translates into roughly three-quarters of the contiguous U.S. Pacific coastline.

Highest Point

Mt. Whitney towers 14,494 feet above sea level, making it the tallest mountain in the lower 48 states.

Lowest Point

Punching in at 282 feet below sea level, California's Death Valley is indeed a deadly place to all but the hardiest. It is also widely considered the lowest place in the Western Hemisphere and one of the hottest places on Earth.

Center Point

The geographic center of California is 38 miles east of the city of Madera.

Major Rivers

Two of California's most important rivers are the Sacramento and the San Joaquin. The Sacramento River, at 382 miles in length, is considered the state's longest river and flows through the northern portion of California's Central Valley. The San Joaquin River is California's second longest river at 330 miles. Its waters are used to irrigate 1500 square miles of farmland on the east side of the Central Valley.

Desert Parkland

Death Valley is an apt name for a corner of the California desert so desolate and barren that only the most hardy can survive. Essentially, the valley floor beneath Telescope Peak, Death Valley is about 300 feet below sea level and covers approximately 3000 square miles. Average yearly precipitation in this arid climate is less than two inches, and temperatures can soar as high as 134°F—the all-time record set in 1913. The park was established on February 11, 1933, and is open year-round, but the weather from October to May usually makes for a nicer visit.

DID YOU  **KNOW?**

The only place in the world that has claimed a higher temperature than Death Valley is Libya. In 1936, it registered a suffocating 136°F.

Trona Pinnacles

In the midst of the California desert, on what was once the bed of Searles Lake, stand more than 500 tufa (calcium carbonate) pinnacles, some rising as high as 140 feet into the sky. These unusual, spiraled towers are thought to have been formed between 10,000 and 100,000 years ago. The 3800-acre area was declared a National Natural Landmark in 1968 and is protected within a Bureau of Land Management Area of Critical Environmental Concern.

If you think the Trona Pinnacles look like something out of a Star Trek movie, you may not be as far off base as you think. The site of these geological wonders is used as a backdrop for as many as 30 film projects annually. Of those, more than a dozen were well-known movie hits, including *The Gate II, Lost in Space, Planet of the Apes* and, of course, *Star Trek V.*

EARTHQUAKE CENTRAL

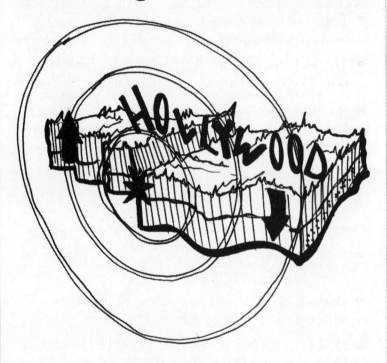

Shake It Up

A lot of people who associate the word "California" with earthquakes have heard of the San Andreas Fault, which runs in a more or less north-south direction through much of the state. However, they may not realize that there are at least 10 other major faults in Southern California alone, as well as hundreds of smaller ones. Southern California sits astride two enormous sections of the earth's crust—the Pacific Plate and the North American Plate. These two plates are actually moving past each other, and about two-thirds of this movement happens on the San Andreas or one of three other parallel faults—the San Jacinto, Elsinore and Imperial faults. These faults are the most dangerous in Southern California and are the cause of about half the significant earthquakes that occur in the area.

- ☞ The first major earthquake of record occurred in 1769 in the Los Angeles region.

- ☞ The San Juan Capistrano earthquake of December 8, 1812, killed 40 people and destroyed the church they were attending.

- ☞ Shockwaves were felt along the San Andreas Fault from Fort Tejon to Los Angeles, San Francisco and Sacramento in January 1857.

- ☞ In October 1868, 30 people were killed when an earthquake in central California shook the Hayward Fault, a main branch of the San Andreas Fault. This earthquake was the first to be called "the great earthquake."

- ☞ In March 1876, an earthquake along the Sierra Nevada fault system killed 27 people and destroyed more than 100 homes.

- ☞ On April 19, 1892, an earthquake damaged or destroyed brick and frame buildings alike in Vacaville.

- ☞ Christmas Day 1899 was a sad one, when an earthquake killed six people and injured several others near San Jacinto.

- ☞ Known as one of the greatest earthquakes ever to hit California, the earthquake of April 18, 1906, killed 700 people. Resulting fires raged throughout San Francisco, and the end cost was estimated at more than $500 million.

- ☞ Several shocks occurring in 1915 in the southern Imperial Valley and at Mexicali, a city just south of the Mexican border, caused six deaths, several injuries and $1 million in property damage.

- ☞ In April 1918, only two buildings were left standing in San Jacinto's business district after an earthquake hit that community.

☞ It may have occurred off the coast, but the earthquake of June 1925 took 13 lives in Santa Barbara and caused $8 million in damage.

☞ The November 1927 earthquake near Lompoc caused damage to hillsides.

☞ In March 1933, Long Beach residents experienced an earthquake that took 115 lives and caused $40 million in property damage.

☞ A May 1940 earthquake in the Imperial Valley and the neighboring Brawley area caused approximately $6 million in structural damage to buildings.

☞ The Kern County earthquake of July 1952 took 12 lives and caused countless injuries and $60 million in property damage.

☞ The 1989 Loma Prieta earthquake collapsed the busy Nimitz Freeway, killing 42 drivers.

☞ The Northridge earthquake devastated the Southland on January 17, 1994. Although it had only a moderate reading on the moment magnitude scale, which has come to be favored over the Richter scale for certain types of measurement, it had the highest ground acceleration in an urban area ever instrumentally recorded in North America. It has so far been the most costly earthquake in U.S. history. The scary part? This major quake happened on a fault that had previously gone undetected.

California records about 500,000 detectable seismic tremors each year.

HUMAN DELINEATIONS

Counties Galore

California boasts 58 counties, but when people talk about Southern California, they generally mean Los Angeles, Santa Barbara, Ventura, Riverside, San Bernardino, San Diego, Orange and Imperial counties, though sometimes San Luis Obispo and Kern counties are thrown in.

County Curiosities

☛ The area may have been explored as early as 1540, and folks settled in the region by 1858, but Imperial County wasn't officially founded until August 7, 1907.

☛ Kern County is California's third largest county and is commonly referred to as "California's Golden Empire."

☛ Los Angeles County is one of the largest counties in the U.S., larger than Delaware and Rhode Island combined.

☛ Silver was discovered in 1887 in the Santa Ana Mountains of Orange County.

☛ Most of the 1234 square miles of Joshua Tree National Park are located in Riverside County.

☛ The ghost town of Calico, located in San Bernardino County, is one the few original mining towns of the Old West still standing.

☛ Father Junipero Serra founded the Mission San Luis Obispo de Tolosa in 1772. The mission, which is located in downtown San Luis Obispo, still operates as a church.

☛ The Santa Barbara County Courthouse, which was dedicated on August 14, 1929, was designed in the style of a Spanish courtyard.

☛ In 1542, the first Europeans arrived in what would come to be known as Ventura County.

WILD IN CALIFORNIA

A Cornucopia of Critters

The unique Southern California bioregion provides habitat to a multitude of creatures. Predators include mountain lions, black bears, coyotes, gray foxes and kit foxes. Other mammals include badgers, mule deer and raccoons. There are many magnificent birds, such as hawks, golden eagles, herons, ospreys and peregrine falcons. The desert is home to iguanas, desert toads and the now-endangered desert tortoise. The coast gives us a variety of seabirds such as the California brown pelican, as well as sea mammals like the California sea lion and California gray whale. Rare animals include the Stephens' kangaroo rat, monarch butterfly, San Diego horned lizard, Peninsular desert bighorn sheep, orange-throated whiptail, California least tern, Belding's savannah sparrow, least Bell's vireo, Santa Ana sucker, arroyo southwestern toad and Tehachapi pocket mouse.

Somebody Save Me!

There are many endangered or threatened California species on both federal and state agency lists. But one heartening thing is that wherever you find a species in peril, you will almost certainly also find a group dedicated to saving it. Even the rather humble Santa Ana sucker, a fish today found in only a very few Southern California rivers, has its very own Santa Ana Sucker Conservation Team. It doesn't have quite the ring of the Bighorn Institute, another hardworking group, but more power to it. The Santa Ana sucker was once one of the most common fish of the Los Angeles Basin's rivers and streams, but it requires clean water to survive and so is a prime indicator of the region's water quality.

Return of the Thunderbird?

The California condor (*Gymnogyps californianus*) is a type of vulture. It is one of the largest flying birds, weighing 18 to 31 pounds and having a wingspan of 9 to 10 feet, and yet it can soar for hours, catching thermal drafts that carry it as high as 15,000 feet. Native American peoples have many legends of the "Thunderbird." They believed that the beating of its huge wings brought thunder to the skies, and naturally, they attributed great power to the bird.

California condors had almost become extinct by 1983, when there were fewer than 30 birds in the wild. However, a corner was turned that year when the Zoological Society of San Diego began the first captive propagation program for condors. As of February 2007, there were 279 California condors, 128 of which live in the wild, mainly in those portions of California and Baja California where they have been reintroduced. Their continued existence depends on protection of their habitat (they are particularly fond of caves and crevices in cliffs), which, like every other place in California, is being steadily encroached upon by humans.

DID YOU KNOW?

California Condors do not have vocal chords, which limits their communication to a series of hisses and grunts. However, they do blush, turning a brighter shade of pink when excited or during the mating season.

Cute, but They're Still Rats

The Stephens' kangaroo rat (*Dipodomys stephensi*) was added to the U.S. Fish and Wildlife Service's Federal Endangered Species list in 1988, and it is also considered a threatened species by the California Department of Fish and Game. It lives in the dry grasslands and scrub of Southern California. Real estate development has shrunk its range dramatically, and the majority of its population now lives in Riverside County. The 1988 listing halted many development projects throughout its range, which of course didn't sit well with many people, who were doubly offended that progress had been brought to a halt for the sake of a rat. However, these creatures are quite endearing. Like all kangaroo rats, they get around by hopping on their long back feet and use their shorter front paws to gather seeds, which they then store in fur-lined, external cheek pouches.

Least but Not Last

The California least tern (*Sterna antillarum*) is one of the smallest members of the tern family. It is gray and white with long, narrow, black-tipped wings and a black cap. Its breeding range once extended along the Southern California coast between Santa Barbara and San Diego, with some nesting as far north as San Francisco and as far south as Baja California, but today, its main habitat is around the San Francisco Bay, with only a few areas along the Southern California coastline. The Pacific Coast Highway cut into much of its nesting habitat and also made human interference easier. Many California least terns have moved their nests farther inland as a result, which unfortunately makes them more vulnerable to fox predation. In 1988, three Orange County tern flocks lost 75 percent of their population to foxes.

DID YOU KNOW?

If the California least tern population does survive, we may have the U.S. Military largely to thank for it. That's because U.S. naval bases and training centers tend to be on remote beaches that are off-limits to the general public. The U.S. Navy and Marine Corps have teamed up with the U.S. Fish and Game Service to manage a large number of these breeding grounds, minimizing human impact. As a result, 600 breeding pairs in 1970 grew to 2300 pairs in 1993. Today, one-third of the California least tern population breeds on Navy or Marine Corps bases.

Sheep Shape

The largest remnant of the Peninsular desert bighorn sheep (*Ovis canadensis nelsoni*), an increasingly rare subspecies of the bighorn sheep, finds its home in Anza-Borrego Desert State Park on the eastern side of San Diego County, which is fitting, as *borrego* is Spanish for "sheep." Bighorn sheep are quite different from the domesticated sheep we are all more familiar with. For one thing, they have hair, not wool. The rams have huge, curling horns, which only grow and curve more as the animals age. Desert bighorns are like camels in their ability to store water for days at a time. They are most comfortable in rocky areas where they can climb to evade their enemies.

Bighorn sheep roamed the Borrego Desert for thousands of years. In the early 1800s, an estimated 1.5 million of them ranged as far south as Baja California. Sadly, today less than three percent of that number remains. There are somewhere in the neighborhood of 200 sheep in the park today. Like other endangered species, the arrival of large members of human settlers harmed the sheep, and they have little or no immunity to many of the diseases carried by livestock.

VARIED VEGETATION

A Plethora of Plants

Containing mountains, coastal land, desert and an enormous central valley, California is the most ecologically diverse state in the country.

About 30 precent of the roughly 5000 species of plant life growing in California are endemic to the state. Most of these rare beauties grow in California because of its unique geological history and climate.

Beauty in Blue
As blue as the California sky and as beautiful a bloom as you've ever seen, the California lilac (*Ceanothus* spp.) grows throughout most of the state. The shrub, which is considered an evergreen and grows to an average height of five feet, usually blooms in May and June, but unless temperatures dip lower than 15°F, it typically remains green year-round.

Rare and Wonderful

The Catalina ironwood (*Lyonothamnus floribundus*) is considered a relic species unique to California. The medium-sized evergreen grows to an average height of 25 to 35 feet and has fernlike leaves and clusters of white blossoms. Twenty thousand years ago it flourished on the mainland, but now it is native only to the islands off the Southern California coast, particularly Catalina Island.

Odd and Obscure

Sand-loving phlox might live smack dab in the middle of the Mojave Desert, but it's only visible in years in which rainfall is higher than average. The ground-hugging cover grows quite sparsely, rather than in obvious bunches, and you actually have to look for it to find it. When there aren't prime growing conditions in a given year, the perennial plant seems to go into a state of hibernation, waiting for just the right time to burst forth in purplish blossoms once again.

Towering Overhead

It may be younger than once thought, but one of the world's most majestic and largest redwoods still calls Sequoia National Park home. General Sherman, a giant sequoia, was so named by James Wolverton, who had served under the famous general during the Civil War. Standing 275 feet tall and measuring 30 feet in diameter at its base, General Sherman was thought to be close to 6000 years old, but today folks at the Western Ecological Research Center estimate its age at closer to 2000 years. Although not the tallest, with 52,000 cubic feet of wood, it ranks by volume as the world's largest tree.

Disappearing Giants

California forests are constantly under attack by urban sprawl. Between 1992 and 1997 alone, 244,000 acres disappeared, adding to the more than 85 percent of original coast redwoods and 70 percent of ancient forests in the Sierra Nevadas that have already been lost.

More Than Just Redwoods

Approximately 35 percent of California is covered in forests. The most densely forested areas are the Klamath Mountains and the Coast Ranges north of San Francisco and the Sierra Nevadas.

POPULATION INFORMATION

Populous California

Estimates place California's 2006 population at 37,172,015, making it the country's most populated state with 12 percent of all Americans calling it home. It is considered the country's 13th fastest-growing state, and it has about four million more residents than all of Canada.

Population Through the Years

Census Year	Population
1850	92,597
1860	379,994
1870	560,247
1880	864,694
1890	1,213,398
1900	1,485,053
1950	10,586,223
2000	33,871,648

Topping the Charts

Eight of California's cities are listed in the country's 50 most populated cities. The 2000 census gives the following estimates for 2005:

☛ Los Angeles, population 3,844,829, in second spot nationally (New York is America's most populated city with 8.1 million residents)

☛ San Diego, population 1,255,540, in eighth position

☛ San Jose, population 912,332, in 10th

☛ San Francisco, population 739,426, in 14th

☛ Long Beach, population 474,014, in 34th

☛ Fresno, population 461,116, in 37th

☛ Sacramento, population 456,441, in 38th

☛ Oakland, population 395,274, in 44th

Overall Distribution

California's population per square mile is 217.6 persons.

California's most populated county is Los Angeles County, with 9,519,338 folks calling it home. Coming in at a very distant second place is Orange County, with 2,846,289 residents.

Men vs. Women

California's population is fairly evenly divided when it comes to men and women. As of 2000, there were 16,996,756 women, equaling 50.2 percent of the population, while men lagged slightly behind at 16,874,892 or 49.8 percent.

Will You Marry Me?

California has the largest number of residents aged 18 years and over of any state—as of the 2000 Census, more than 26 million. Of that number, 7,843,907 have never been married, 13,657,201 are currently married, 642,670 are separated, 2,474,567 have been divorced and 1,457,818 have been widowed.

DID YOU KNOW?

Most Californians fall in the 25 to 54 age range, with the average age being 33.3 years. However, with more than 3.8 million residents aged 65 and older (based on 2003 population estimates), California has a higher number of seniors than any other state.

CALIFORNIA MELTING POT

Ethnic Diversity

According to the 2000 Census, less than half of Californians were white American or non-Hispanic white. This was the first recorded statistic (except for Hawaii) of a white minority in any U.S. state. Here's what the overall population breakdown looks like, based on 2005 estimates:

Race	Percentage of Population
White (non-Hispanic)	43.8
Hispanic or Latino	35.2
Asian/Pacific Islander	12.3
African-American	6.2
American Indian/Alaskan Native	0.5
Persons of two or more racial backgrounds	2.0

Mother Tongue

The 2000 Census points out that 60.5 percent of California residents speak English at home. Of the more than 200 languages spoken and read in California, Spanish is the second most popular language of choice, spoken by 25.8 percent of residents, and is considered the state's "alternative language." Chinese is the language of choice for 2.6 percent, Tagalog for 2.5 percent and Vietnamese for 1.3 percent of the population. California is considered one of the most linguistically diverse areas in the world.

Religious Diversity

While New Age and eastern philosophies are gaining notoriety in California, most residents still declare themselves Christians. Here's a look at the statistics:

Faith or Denomination	Percentage
Christian	
Protestant	39.4
Catholic	32.0
Mormon	1.6
Other Christian	1.7
Jewish	2.9
Muslim	0.8
Other	2.6
Unaffiliated	19.0

WHERE THE MONEY IS... AND WHERE IT'S NOT

Standard of Living

The high cost of living in certain cities definitely limits who lives there. California has communities with the highest average per capita income of just about anywhere on Earth, while at the other end of the spectrum, it has places with some of the lowest per capita incomes of any First World country. Here's the breakdown, by city, per year.

Wealthiest California Cities

City	County	Income
Belvedere	Marin	$113,595
Rancho Santa Fe	San Diego	$113,132
Atherton	San Mateo	$112,408
Rolling Hills	Los Angeles	$111,031
Woodside	San Mateo	$104,667

Poorest Southern California Cities

City	County	Income
Mecca	Riverside	$6,389
Mettler	Kern	$6,919
Winterhaven	Imperial	$7,220
Palo Verde	Imperial	$7,250
Coachella	Riverside	$7,416
Arvin	Kern	$7,480

ROADSIDE ATTRACTIONS

Romantic Route 66

What started out as a way to meet the practical need of connecting Chicago, Illinois, and the seemingly endless small towns along the way to Los Angeles, California, turned into a piece of American history and has as many legends as bends and curves. But Route 66 is no longer part of the United States Highway System, having been decommissioned in 1985.

Waste Not, Want Not

If you're traveling through Helendale on Route 66, you can't miss this unique roadside attraction. Artist Elmer Long created his forest of bottle trees, lovingly referred to by visitors and locals alike as Elmer's Place. He used recycled bottles for leaves and branches, then slipped them onto iron rods and other metal objects that he welded to an iron trunk. His unique form of art has been highlighted in *USA Today*, *The Press-Enterprise* and even *Lonely Planet*. Well, with 200-plus bottle trees, I guess you can't help but get noticed!

Fascinating Fruit

A giant orange crafted into a roadside stand graces a corner of Foothill Boulevard in Fontana. Roadside stands like this one were at one time quite common and served up orange juice that was so sweet it seemed the oranges had been freshly plucked from nearby groves and hand-squeezed on the premises. Today, though orange groves no longer stretch for miles around, Bono's Historic 66 Orange Stand—the last of its kind—remains.

Don't Jerk My Leg!

Jerky lovers everywhere should know about this roadside stop. Located on Baker Boulevard in Baker, a restaurant known as Alien Fresh Jerky sells everything from teriyaki beef jerky to salmon and clam varieties. They even sell stuffed olives, pistachios and almonds, and if you're just not sure what you're craving, they provide samples.

Ostrich, You Say?

Feel like a snack of ostrich jerky? Or perhaps you're looking for an ostrich-themed gift for that special someone? Located 40 miles north of Santa Barbara, Ostrich Land sells ostrich eggs, both painted and unpainted, as well as ostrich and emu jerky.

Dying for a Donut

If you've a sweet tooth and donuts are your thing, California has at least a couple of donut holes to die for. Randy's Donuts, on Manchester Boulevard in Inglewood, is quite easy to find. Built in 1952, the donut diner features a giant donut on its roof. Aside from its one-of-a-kind appearance, the company produces taste-tempting baked goods in both sweet and savory varieties.

The Donut Hole, in La Puente, is another unmistakable Californian landmark. It was built in either 1958 or 1968, depending on the source, and patrons can actually drive through a donut hole, place and pick up their order inside, and continue out another donut hole.

Top Notch

The Kansas City Barbeque in San Diego not only boasts top-of-the-line vittles, it offers a lot to talk about during your dining experience. The restaurant, which really isn't all that big, boasts several extensive and unique collections. There are more than 350 hats attached to one side of the ceiling rafters, a collection of more than 400 state and country license plates, 15 fully operational life preservers donated by various branches of the U.S. military and the Canadian navy, and an assortment of bras that apparently, with great mystery, hang themselves from lights and rafters during the night shift. According to the company website, the largest bra in the collection is a Zorina 64FF. The smallest obviously pales in comparison. This unique stopover was chosen as a filming location for the 1986 Tom Cruise movie *Top Gun*.

Nothin' like Country

Country music lovers can have all their needs met and enjoy some good old-fashioned country music while they're at it. Buck Owens' Crystal Palace in Bakersfield is really an all-inclusive, one-stop deal. The brainchild of Buck Owens himself, the Crystal Palace serves up a mean menu and, occasionally, live country music. There's also an on-site music museum full of Buck Owens memorabilia, a music vault and a gift shop.

Truly Something for Everyone

Located on Pearblossom Highway, just out of Littlerock, Charlie Brown Farms is a favorite stop for Southern California travelers headed to or from Las Vegas or the ski slopes. Whether because of the old-time friendly atmosphere or the many unusual items that can be purchased, many motorists find it irresistible. There aren't too many places in the world where you can buy chocolate-covered ants (or one of a thousand other kinds of candy), rattlesnake meat and an Elvis statue and then head on over to the Gnome Village or the House of Dolls and pick out something to add to your collection. The restaurant serves a variety of exotic meats—there's barbecued buffalo, ostrich and even venison on a skewer.

A Remnant of Old Oceanside

If you're in the neighborhood of Oceanside on Highway 101, consider taking afternoon tea at 101 Café. Touted as Oceanside's oldest café, the diner has been serving up good old-fashioned, homemade grub (including their all-day breakfast) since it opened its doors in 1928. Back then, the café was just a small, 20-seat

TOURISM: ATTRACTIONS GALORE

establishment. Today it's three times the size and has retained the drive-in addition, complete with rolling carhops, from the 1950s.

"Dream as if You'll Live Forever. Live as if You'll Die Today."
That's a quote from legendary actor James Dean, whose roadside memorial at Cholame/Shandon is a touching tribute to the young actor who died nearby in a car accident on September 30, 1955. The memorial, a concrete and stainless steel structure built in Japan and donated by Seita Ohnishi, was placed around a "tree of heaven" near the Cholame post office in 1977. The story goes that Seita was a fan and, on his visit to the site years before, was troubled by the lack of an appropriate memorial. The nearby junction of Highway 41 and Highway 48 was named the James Dean Memorial Junction on September 30, 2005, the 50th anniversary of his death. The adjacent restaurant also boasts a collection of James Dean memorabilia for visitors to enjoy while dining.

Holy Spelunkers, Robin! Have We Found the Bat Cave?
Bronson Canyon is an interesting site hidden away in L.A.'s Griffith Park and is quite well known by student filmmakers for miles around. Known as Bronson Caves, the tunnels dug out of what was once a rock quarry are not at all the makings of Mother Nature. The stories surrounding their origin are wide and varied. The use of these tunnels in movies and television is quite well documented; they are featured in at least 55 movies and 17 television series, including *Batman, Little House on the Prairie, Gunsmoke, Bonanza* and various adventures of many of the *Star Trek* series.

Desert Dinosaurs

What better place to park odd, old and redundant aircraft than in the middle of the Mojave Desert? A collection of about 200 obsolete remnants is parked in a fenced-off area just outside the Mojave Airport. And though you can somewhat see them from the highway, a fence and foot patrol surrounds these gigantic remains, separating them from a curious public. Still, passersby do attempt to sneak up for a closer look and to snap a couple of photos from the fence line. Some of these planes may eventually be serviced and resurrected, but most will die a natural death. Some have called this the largest "graveyard" of its kind in existence.

Making the Destination

The sign announcing the town of Felicity gives an elevation number, but no population. That's because this town, known as the "Official Center of the World," is really just a collection of monuments heralding the history of the world. Everything from a replica of one of the pyramids to the Eiffel Tower stairs and a granite wall honoring the Marine Corps Korean War veterans can be found on a short walking tour of the site.

Although the first white settler passed through the area in 1540, and it was a regular stop on the mule train mail route of the mid-1800s, Felicity wasn't legally established until March 1986.

DID YOU KNOW?

How does a town become the Official Center of the World? Apparently just by declaration. Jacques-Andre Istel had only been mayor of Felicity for a few months when the idea came to him. Although he admits that people have always thought he was crazy, he has succeeded in getting Imperial County to support the claim, as well as the Institut Géographique National of France and, we kid you not, the People's Republic of China.

The Wild, Hollywood West

Tucked away near the Yucca Valley is an authentic western town called Pioneertown. Built in 1946, the town was originally used as the backdrop for several Hollywood westerns starring elite actors such as Gene Autry, Roy Rogers and others. Its location made it prudent to include an on-site residence for the stars and others involved in these filmmaking projects. And today, the

town—including an authentic western hotel, eating establishments, original residences and other lodgings, all ready to serve—is open to the public.

Have Boot, Will Travel

Quality Shoe Service on Santa Monica Boulevard in Los Angeles not only offers top-notch service, but also has two very innovative mascots: a black minivan converted into a cowboy boot and another vehicle converted into a hiking boot. Both were created by a metal worker—the hiking boot about 20 years ago and the cowboy boot fairly recently.

Mountainous Memorabilia

Although military enthusiasts will have no doubt heard of Fort Irwin, the rest of us may need a refresher. The Mojave tribe was believed to have inhabited this area as far back as 15,000 years ago. More recently, Spanish explorer Father Francisco Barces traveled the nearby Mojave Indian Trail in 1796, and in 1826, American explorer Jedediah Smith spent some time there trapping for fur. But it wasn't until 1844 that Captain John C. Fremont, the first member of the U.S. military to visit the area, established a camp there, and Fort Irwin was born. The post was opened and closed numerous times until 1979, when the government chose it as the site for the National Training Center. The first batch of trainees passed through its doors in 1981, and the base continues to be active to this day.

So why the history lesson? Because if you happen to pass by, you may notice a rather unique and colorful pile of boulders. This mountain of rock has been transformed by years worth of trainees marking their stay with personalized graffiti. In a way, it's a pictorial history of the area—and quite a sight at that!

An Ode to Bubblegum

This one will leave you with something to chew on. Back in 1960, folks in San Luis Obispo began to notice, and complain about, chewed bubblegum stuck on the two cement walls lining an alley in downtown Obispo. Initially, attempts were made to remove the nuisance, but to no avail. Shortly after cleaning, there were always new additions to the walls. Townsfolk gave in, and today there are millions of wads of chewed gum stuck on those two walls. Ick!

How Hot Is It?

It's 134 feet tall and flashes the current temperature at anyone who's interested. Arguably one of the world's largest thermometers, this giant was constructed in 1991 and is located in Baker. Now, I bet you were wondering why it's 134 feet tall. Apparently, the height represents the highest temperature ever recorded in nearby Death Valley—and, in fact, the highest temperature ever recorded in North America—back in 1913.

Saved from the Salvage Heap

It's a good thing folks in Oxnard carry their Christmas spirit year-round. Without it, a 22-foot Santa statue that once graced the town's Santa Claus Lane would have been nothing more than a pile of rubble. Apparently, the old fellow was looking worse for wear and was, no doubt, a disturbing site for area youngsters. But just before he was scheduled for demolition, area locals gathered together to refurbish the plaster Christmas icon with a coat of fresh paint. Today, he's regained his dignity and proudly sits facing northbound traffic on Highway 101.

Love Those Lemons

The community of Lemon Grove, population 26,000 and incorporated in 1977, is proud of its motto: "Best Climate on Earth." According to visitors, it can also boast having the world's largest lemon, with its lemon mascot perched in the city's downtown core.

According to the *Guinesses Book of World Records*, the skinniest house in the world measures 10 feet wide and 50 feet long. Nelson Rummond built the house in Long Beach in the 1930s to accommodate his long, skinny lot. People live there, so you can't look inside, but seeing it from the street will likely leave you wondering how they manage to do it.

Big Boulder

Landers might be a town with a modest population of 2400, give or take a few, but it has a lot to talk about. Just outside of town is what's known as Giant Rock. Standing about seven stories tall and occupying roughly 5800 square feet of ground, Giant Rock is not only famed as the world's largest freestanding boulder (before 2000, when a third of the rock split off from the rest, that is), it's also considered a holy site by Native Americans. It also, coincidentally, is considered a prime destination for UFOs and was the site of several UFO conventions until well into the 1970s. Today, it remains an interesting roadside attraction.

DID YOU KNOW?

World-famous San Diego Zoo houses more than 4000 animals of 800 species.

CALIFORNIA DREAMIN'

Maybe He Had Instructions from On High

"The Integratron" was designed by an engineer, stands 38 feet tall, has a 50-foot diameter and is used as a "rejuvenation and time machine." To say the 16-sided, wooden dome structure near Landers—which well-known pilot and UFO abductee George Van Tassel first began constructing in 1954 but didn't quite finish before his death in 1978—was a mammoth undertaking is an understatement. The quality of construction was critical to the success of Van Tassel's experiment, and the mathematical calculations required to determine the perfect site in relation to Egypt's Great Pyramid and Giant Rock were onerous. Still, despite the fact that Van Tassel didn't see the finished product he so dreamed about, visitors to the site say they experience interesting sound phenomena and other energy forces.

DID YOU KNOW?

Before his death, George Van Tassel wrote six books on his extraterrestrial experiences and garnered 11,000 followers to attend his UFO conferences.

Talk About Recycling

Just off Highway 5 near Coalinga, the remnants of a once prosperous oil industry have been transformed into imaginative creatures that look a little like Pez dispensers. Coalinga is a relatively small community with a population of about 15,000, and among its fine residents is one Jean Dakessian Jones. The local artist thought decorating the pumping units might liven up the dry, barren landscape a little and bring visitors into the nearby motel she owned with her husband. She approached Shell Oil, the company who owned the pumps, and was not only granted permission, but the company also donated the paint required for the job.

In 1973, Jean transformed 23 pumps into elaborate creatures—zebras, butterflies, giraffes, whatever caught her fancy at the moment—creating what came to be known as the Iron Zoo in the process. Although the creatures have been thinned out over the years, as pumps have been taken out of service, travelers can still catch a glimpse of the few that remain. And a handful of interested residents have considered acquiring the removed pumps and bringing them home. So keep your eyes open. The Iron Zoo might be resurrected to its glory days before you know it!

"All the World's a Stage"

What began with a little girl's dream to dance has taken Marta Becket from the glitz and glam of Radio City Music Hall and Broadway to a small, unobtrusive opera house in Death Valley Junction. Marta, a professional ballerina, arrived in what was no more than a ghost town in 1967, looking for a garage or a mechanic to fix a flat tire. She strolled along the mostly empty streets until she happened upon a theater. She couldn't believe her luck, and the next day, she and her husband approached the town manager with an offer to rent the property. She renamed it the Amargosa Opera House, got busy with renovations and repairs and held her first performance on February 10, 1968, to a total attendance of 12.

But numbers weren't important to Marta. At times, no one came to see her dance. So, in her characteristically optimistic fashion, she simply went to work painting an audience on the walls of the theater. It took her four years to complete these murals, which today draw as much interest as her weekly performances. Marta's dream was to dance her own dances and create her own stories, and to date, regardless of the hardships she's had to overcome throughout the years, she's done just that. In the process, her energy and enthusiasm for her art has proven somewhat contagious. Today, Death Valley Junction is not only a tourist destination, but also a haven for artists of all mediums.

My Home, My…Ship?

Maybe it's because the city of Encinitas, population 58,000, is located on the coast that this story doesn't seem all that odd… really. Still, this one might even give the Biblical Noah cause to pause.

If you stroll along Third Street you may think you've come upon a marooned ship or two. These two "ships" are actually houses constructed with discarded and reused lumber from a hotel that was torn down back in 1910. The owner at the time was Miles Minor Kellogg, and in 1928, he decided to recycle the wood by building a house. But Kellogg's inventiveness took the idea to an entirely different level, and his finished products must have left townsfolk scratching their heads. Even stalwart seamen have to take a second look when first coming upon the site.

One Way to do a Little Branding

For Leslie Brand, 31 acres nestled at the base of the Verdugo Mountains in Glendale was a sanctuary of sorts. The surrounding wilderness provided peace, solitude and endless opportunities for hiking and general exploring—a wonderful place for him and his family to enjoy. Thankfully, Leslie was as generous as he was appreciative of his land. He died in 1925 and bequeathed his estate to the City of Glendale on the death of his wife with the provision that his home, El Miradaro, built in 1904, be transformed into a public library and that the rest of the land be protected as parkland. Since 1956, the Brand Library and Brand Park, and later Brand Studios (an art gallery) and assorted other amenities, have been available for the public to enjoy.

DID YOU KNOW?

A 1993 article in the *Glendale News Press* unveiled several accounts of ghostly activity at the Brand Library. Cool drafts, shadowy figures, moaning voices—staff members have reported these and many other strange occurrences. When asked who they think the ghost might be, they all seem to point the finger in the same direction: Mr. Leslie Brand. After all, he died in the building that was constructed to his specifications. Why would he ever want to leave?

A Retreat Worthy of the Bard

Out in Santiago Canyon near Lake Forest lies the house of Madame Helena Modjeska, arguably the most famous Polish actress in history. She and her husband, Count Chlapowski, and friends hit upon the idea of starting a utopian agricultural venture in Anaheim. When that didn't work out, she began her U.S. acting career, touring the country as an acclaimed Shakespearean actress, though she never lost her Polish accent. When they were not on tour, she and the Count retreated to Arden, the mansion they had commissioned architect Stanford White to build for them among the California live oaks. They lived there from 1888 to 1906, when they retired to Newport Beach. The house has since been named a national historic monument, one of only two in Orange County.

One Man's Junk...

Lonely Planet calls this attraction in Watts, Los Angeles, the "world's strangest salute to trash." Back in 1921, Simon Rodia decided to recycle the junk in his backyard into a unique collection of towers. For more than 33 years he welded and crafted an assortment of one-of-a-kind towers, some 100 feet tall. Then, one day, he deeded his property to his neighbors and disappeared. After much dispute and a series of strength tests to determine if the structures were safe and could withstand the forces of nature, the City of Los Angeles took over the property. Today, Watts Junk Towers is open to the public and has been the topic of at least one documentary.

Shouldn't That Have Been "Burrow"?

For 38 years, beginning in 1906 (or 1902, depending on the source), William Henry "Burro" Schmidt spent much of his time tunneling a total of 2087 feet into Copper Mountain in the Mojave Desert. He blasted through the solid rock, removing the rubble by wheelbarrow or on his back, day after day from fall until summer, when he would work as a ranch hand. But he never really explained why he was doing this. After all, the tunnel merely opens on the other side of the mountain to a 4000-foot drop. Eventually, Burro and a partner named Mike Lee took visitors on tours of the tunnel, but both fellows died before the mystery of "why" had been solved.

Desert Devotion

Cue part two. After the deaths of Burro and Mike, Evelyn Tonie Seger and her husband purchased the land. Their main struggle wasn't burrowing through a mountain—it was hauling water. Shortly after the couple purchased the land, Evelyn found her husband sprawled on the ground near death. He begged Evelyn to honor his last wish—to find a water source near their new home. In the Mojave Desert, you may be wondering? Wonderful wife that she was, she actually managed to do just that.

Evelyn died in 2003. Since then, access to the land and the Burro Schmidt Tunnels is administered through the Bureau of Land Management Ridgecrest Resource Area.

A MYRIAD OF MUSEUMS

The Human and Not-So-Human Family

The San Diego Museum of Man treats visitors to all the bells and whistles of other well-endowed museums, but has taken great pains to provide an extra-critical focus on the development of humankind. Among its permanent exhibits is "Footsteps Through Time: Four Million Years of Human Evolution." Here, visitors can see how the human physical form has changed throughout the years and compare their hands, feet and even brains with those of other primates. You'll learn how to conduct a proper archaeological dig and catch a glimpse of what we humans might look like in the future. And according to some visitors, the museum also boasts a collection of the macabre— shrunken heads, mummified corpses and the lot.

Rock With a View

The Desert View Tower, a four-story cut-rock foundation located on In-Ko-Pah Road three miles east of Jacumba, overlooks the Imperial Valley at an elevation of 3000 feet above sea level. Jacumba's one-time owner Bert Vaughn built it in the 1920s to honor the area's pioneers. The tower doubles as a museum featuring Native American artifacts and other Americana, and an observation platform offers a view not to be missed.

Going Bananas

Everything in life has its own trivia, and believe it or not, bananas are no exception. The International Banana Club Museum, which started out in 1976 and currently has 17,000 pieces of banana paraphernalia, has the dubious distinction of being the "world's largest collection devoted to any one fruit," according to the *Guinness Book of World Records*. Located in Hesperia, this museum is definitely the place to be if you're looking to go bananas.

What a Lemon!

Being known for its lemons is what put Corona on the map. At the beginning of the 20th century, citrus trees were the target crop produced by new settlers. And by 1913, the town's 5000 acres of groves had earned the reputation of shipping more fruit than any other town in Southern California, making lemons and all things citrus the backbone of the local economy until well into the later part of the 20th century. Today, the Corona Heritage Park and Museum, built in 1937, heralds its proud history in the citrus industry. It even boasts a Sunkist lemon juicer collection!

Weird and Wonderful

Did you ever think you'd see a carving of Pope John Paul II in the eye of a needle? For this and all things odd and creepy, take a trip to the Museum of Jurassic Technology. Located on Venice Boulevard in Culver City, in the Palms district of Los Angeles, the museum's website states that it houses a "specialized repository of relics and artifacts from the Lower Jurassic, with an emphasis on those that demonstrate unusual or curious technological qualities." Hmmm. Well, the fact that someone actually managed to carve a pope in the eye of a needle qualifies as demonstrating "unusual or curious technological qualities."

At the same time, how does an exhibit on trailer park culture, "Garden of Eden on Wheels," qualify? And according to visitors' comments, curious folk who stop by here say the museum is an experience like no other.

STOP!

It's little more than a garage, really, but for automotive enthusiasts, the Museum of Traffic Control and Signal Garden in Fullerton is a green light! Owner and curator John Rietveld has collected more than 80 traffic lights (many that still work) and 650 road signs. While this must-see STOP is the real deal, you do have to make an appointment in advance to view the site.

Roadside Exotica

The world of burlesque might be foreign to many of us, but you'll find yourself quite knowledgeable on the topic after you tour Exotic World, a one-of-a-kind museum to be sure. Dedicated solely to preserving the history of burlesque, the museum is located in Helendale in the one-time home of exotic dancer Jennie Lee. Today, the site is owned and operated by retired dancer Dixie Evans.

How Do You Really Feel?

This is most definitely a stop that will challenge your perceptions. Psychiatry: An Industry of Death is a museum owned and operated by the Citizens Commission on Human Rights, an anti-psychiatry organization that was founded by the Church of Scientology. The exhibit, located on Hollywood's Sunset Boulevard, opened its doors to the public in December 2005 with all the glitz and glam of Hollywood—and a few of its celebrities. The museum is free of charge to the public, and along with an assortment of exhibits, more than a dozen documentaries can be viewed. The museum is already well known for the statistical claims it makes, many of which are quite controversial.

Looking for a Ride?

From tanks and armored personnel carriers to motorcycles, helicopters and anti-tank guns, the Military Vehicle Museum in South El Monte has it all. Established as a non-profit organization back in 1962, the small museum operates largely through volunteers and kind donations. Located about 15 minutes from downtown Los Angeles, the outdoor museum is open to the public on Friday, Saturday and Sunday year-round.

Not So Top-Secret Anymore

Airplane enthusiasts will no doubt enjoy a visit to Blackbird Airpark, a three-acre park located at the Air Force Flight Test Center Museum at Edwards Air Force Base in Palmdale. The park's main features are none other than the mysterious Lockheed SR-71A, the A-12, the U-2D and the one-time top-secret D-21 Drone—all members of the Blackbird family of planes. Plans are in the works to surround the displays with a commemorative wall highlighting all aspects of the history of this family of military aircraft.

All Things Auto

The Petersen Automotive Museum lies right on the corner of Fairfax and Wilshire, a four-story homage to L.A.'s love of the automobile. Originally housed at the Natural History Museum of Los Angeles County when it opened in 1994, the automotive museum moved into the former Ohrbach's department store. The first floor holds a lifelike diorama, where visitors can walk through the history of the automobile, beginning with a facsimile of the 1901 blacksmith shop where the first automobile in L.A. was built, and continuing on through a 1939 car showroom and past a California Highway Patrolman hiding behind a period piece billboard. Upstairs are rotating exhibits of celebrities' cars, and cars that are celebrities in their own right. There's also a hands-on children's area where kids learn how an automotive engine works.

DID YOU KNOW?

The Petersen Automotive Museum holds the sad distinction of being the last place that rapper Notorious B.I.G. was seen alive. He had been there for the Soul Train Awards party on March 9, 1997, and was gunned down at a stoplight shortly after he drove away from the building. His murder remains unsolved to this day.

Hoppily Ever After

What started out as a way to say "I love you" has blossomed into a world-renowned home museum and *Guinness Book of World Records* entry! Candace Frazee and Steve Lubanski met in the summer of 1992. The following Valentine's Day, Steve gave Candace a plush, white bunny sporting a loving message—an idea spurred on by the fact that Candace called Steve her "Hunny Bunny"—and voilá, a tradition was born. From that day on, the couple exchanged a bunny token of some kind every holiday or special event. Now, they do so on a daily basis. In the process, they've transformed their home into a showcase of more than 21,000 bunnies and counting, including a few real ones, and have opened their doors to the public since 1998. The museum, located on Jefferson Drive in Pasadena, is open year-round by appointment only. Candace and Steve also host open houses on all holidays.

The Movieland Wax Museum of Buena Park was open for 43 years, but closed it doors on October 31, 2005. Many of the 300 wax figures were sent to other museums, including the Wax Museum at Fisherman's Wharf. Some, however, were publicly auctioned: the cast of *Star Trek* for $34,000, Elizabeth Taylor/Cleopatra for $25,000 and Elvis for $14,000, to name a few bank-busters.

IS THERE A THEME HERE?

More than Just Berries

Knott's Berry Farm, located in Buena Park, began as a modest family venture with 20 acres of rented land and a dream to grow berries and other produce. The entrepreneurial spirit of Walter and Cordelia Knott, who by 1927 owned two 10-acre lots, propelled the couple into more than simply growing and selling produce. In the true spirit of diversification, Walter developed a new berry he named the boysenberry (a cross between a loganberry, red raspberry and blackberry), while Cordelia was busy baking biscuits, making jellies and operating an on-site tea room that eventually served an assortment of lunch items. On a whim, Cordelia cooked up eight fried chicken dinners and served them to her guests as a special treat one June day in 1934. It cost each patron 65 cents a plate, probably decent coin back in the Dirty Thirties. But the customers came back and brought their friends, who told their friends, and before long, Mrs. Knott's Chicken Dinner Restaurant—a huge, 900-seat venture—was born.

By 1940, Cordelia was serving as many as 4000 chicken dinners on a Sunday. With crowds that large looking to fill their tummies—and recognizing that their restaurant couldn't seat that many at a time—the Knotts decided to give their patrons something to do while they waited. And so the Ghost Town, the first of six theme parks to be erected over the years, was built. Today, visitors can tour the Ghost Town, the Fiesta Village, the Boardwalk, Camp Snoopy, Wild Water Wilderness and Indian Trails, and ride a few of the 37 rides on the current 160-acre site. And of course, there's always a fresh chicken dinner waiting when you're done! Cordelia Knott died in 1974, and Walter passed away in 1981, but the legacy of Knott's Berry Farm continues to the present day with efforts from the current owners.

Knott's Berry Farm was the first theme park in the U.S. and is the 12th most visited amusement park in the country.

The World in Plastic

LEGO has been all the rage with youngsters since Ole Kirk Christiansen began his toy-making business in Billund, Denmark, in 1932. The product didn't always look the way it does today. In fact, the plastic bricks evolved over the years just as the designs have done. But the craze was so all-encompassing that by 1968, LEGOLAND in Billund had opened its doors, and 31 years later, California followed suit with a variation of its own in Carlsbad. LEGOLAND California is located on 128 acres. The theme park's more than 50 rides and numerous hands-on attractions and shows are geared to youngsters aged two to 12. The Carlsbad location is one of only three such theme parks worldwide.

DID YOU KNOW?

The term "Lego" is a contraction of the Danish words *leg godt*, meaning "play well." In Latin, *lego* means, "I put together" or "I assemble."

Wonder if There's Room for a Trivialand— Disneyland Trivia

- The first Tinkerbell was actually a 71-year-old Hungarian circus performer named Tiny Kline.

- Yes, there really is a basketball court tucked away inside the Matterhorn.

- Only 365 days passed from the time ground was broken to the time of Disneyland's opening.

- Maybe that's why opening day—July 17, 1955—was a disaster. Because of a heat wave, the new asphalt hadn't properly dried, allowing women's heels to sink into the pavement. Rides broke down, and on top of everything else, there was a plumber's strike. Walt Disney had to choose between toilets and drinking fountains for the masses. He chose the toilets. As he explained later, "People can buy Pepsi-Cola, but they can't pee in the streets." Not on Main Street anyway.

- Vegetation was a little sparse on opening day as well. Walt had the gardening staff cover up the bare patches with weeds and give them fancy horticultural names.

- Cats like Disneyland, too. Feral cats, anyway. Over 100 were found to be living in Sleeping Beauty's Castle when the walk-through attraction was added, and the workers at this attraction often complained about all the fleas! The cats still take over the park at night, after the visitors leave. Apparently no one minds, because they help control the rat population.

- On July 17, 1995, the 40th anniversary of the park's opening, a time capsule, or "Time Castle," as its plaque is inscribed, was buried in the forecourt of Sleeping Beauty's Castle. It contains memorabilia and messages to future generations.

- Walt did have a small studio above the firehouse on Main Street, which he kept for his personal use. A light is kept lit in the window as a kind of memorial to him.

- Disneyland cost $17 million to build in 1955, which would amount to about $116 million today.

- Ron Dominguez grew up on one of the original Anaheim orange groves that Walt Disney purchased to build the park. Dominguez started as a ticket-taker on opening day and spent his entire working career at the park, ending up as a top executive.

- Tomorrowland was originally set in the then vastly futuristic year of 1986, when Halley's Comet was due to make a reappearance. Even at the beginning though, Walt worried that Tomorrowland would be out of date by the time it was constructed.

- There were many gadgets in Monsanto's House of the Future, but none was more impressive to visitors than the microwave oven. Apparently no one could believe it would ever be possible to bake a potato in just three minutes.

- Walt Disney originally wanted live animals on the Jungle Cruise, until it was pointed out that most such animals would either hide from human visitors or be sleeping during the hours of park operation.

- When it opened in 1967, Pirates of the Caribbean used real skeletons from the UCLA Medical Center because state-of-the-art models didn't look real enough. Thankfully, these remains were eventually returned and given a proper burial.

- The Disney-Alweg Monorail was the first daily run monorail in the entire Western Hemisphere.

- No alcohol is served within Disneyland's gates—except for one place. In New Orleans Square, there is a door marked

"33" that leads to a very exclusive and very pricey club. If you can swing the initiation fee of $8000 to $27,000, and then the steep yearly fees of $4000 to $15,000, that would allow you to buy a drink in Disneyland—once you make it to the top of the waiting list, that is, which is reputed to be seven years long.

☛ While we're talking about New Orleans Square, the telegraph at the railroad station there is actually tapping out a real message. It is Walt's opening day speech. In the early days, the telegraph is said to have tapped out a somewhat risqué message, until Walt mentioned that his wife understood Morse code, upon which the message was quickly changed.

☛ Walt Disney is not cryogenically frozen and ready to be re-animated at some future date, as many would like to believe. At his own request, when he died on December 15, 1966, he was cremated and laid to rest in Forest Lawn Cemetery.

☛ Disneyland's fans don't give up their favorites easily. There is at least one website devoted to "Yesterland," where fans can revisit and then discuss all of Disneyland's discontinued attractions.

GHOSTLY ENCOUNTERS

Hotel Haunting

The Hotel del Coronado is believed to be haunted by the ghost of Kate Morgan. The young woman checked into the establishment in 1892 to wait for her husband. Her lifeless body was discovered just outside the building, a victim of an apparent suicide. Strange happenings have been documented ever since, and more than 37 paranormal readings have been recorded in her hotel room.

Famed Fellows

The Beverly Hills Hotel on Sunset Boulevard claims to have a few famous paranormal guests. Among them are Sergei Rachmaninoff and Harpo Marx.

Ship of Ghouls

Once a beautiful luxury ship only the elite could afford to travel on, the 1000-foot HMS *Queen Mary* now sits in Long Beach Harbor. Built in the 1930s, the ship first set sail in 1936 and continued transporting the rich and famous to vacation destinations until the start of World War II. Luxury travel was suspended during the war years, and the *Queen Mary* shifted clientele, transporting troops first, and later war brides and their children. After the war, she returned to her original purpose as a cruise ship. The *Queen Mary* was eventually sold to the City of Long Beach and transformed into a maritime museum and hotel. Today, the ship is said to be one of the most haunted places in the world. As many as 150 individual spirits are said to wander the floating hotel, appearing from time to time to the many guests who flock there from around the world. An eerie vacation choice, to be sure.

Maybe It's Not Just a Ride...

It might be a theme park, but Disneyland's Haunted Mansion is just one of the park's many attractions believed to be truly haunted. Depending on the source (Disney itself acknowledges these stories but says they are fiction), three ghosts call the mansion home. Visitors have reported having their hair pulled, being touched on their backs, hearing footsteps and seeing a face peer from the grand staircase. Another ghost reportedly roaming the park near the Pirates of the Caribbean ride is believed to be that of a young boy. He began haunting the park after his mother, wanting to give her young son one last gift after his death, decided to spread his ashes near his favorite ride. Sadly, his spirit doesn't seem to be at rest because he's been seen from time to time crying. Numerous other ghosts have also been reported, but your best bet is to visit Disneyland and decide for yourself if the rumors are true, or if they're just that—rumors!

Old Faithful

Talk about a friend for life. The *Bakersfield Californian* building on Eye Street in Bakersfield is believed to be haunted by the ghost of a German shepherd dog. Yup, he's faithfully waiting for his beloved master to show up and take him home.

Lickin' for Love in All the Wrong Places

Folks visiting the Los Angeles Pet Cemetery may find themselves being licked by the ghost of Rudolf Valentino's dog. It's believed the dog, which was buried at the cemetery back in 1929, likes to lick people who wander near his grave!

Dangerous Drive?

An old carriage pulled by white horses and carrying the ghost of Harry Houdini is believed to haunt Laurel Canyon and Lookout Mountain Drive near Hollywood. Reports of these and other apparitions are believed to be the cause of many car accidents in the area.

One Sad Song

Rock star Gram Parsons of 1960s group The Byrds died of an overdose in room 8 of the Joshua Tree Inn. According to many who've stayed in that room, his ghost is far from at rest. Objects moving and shaking for no apparent reason are just a few of the many reported phenomena.

Wandering Spirit

The twists and turns that characterize Channel Street in Sanger have led to it more commonly being referred to as Snake Road. On a stretch of the road near the Kings River, the ghost of a grieving woman is said to wander. The story goes that the woman was traveling with her two daughters and lost control of her car. Her daughters were thrown from the vehicle as it crashed into the nearby river, but the mother was trapped. It is believed her ghost is still searching for her daughters, who, sadly, were flung into the powerful river and drowned, their bodies carried many miles away.

Like Clockwork

For no apparent reason, a lady in pink haunts the Yorba Family Cemetery in Yorba Linda. However, she is only spotted on the night of June 15, and only every other year. She must not seem threatening because locals are said to gather at the appropriate time to keep watch around the cemetery, hoping to catch a glimpse of her.

COMMUNITY FOUNDATIONS

Founding Fathers...or, in Some Cases, Padres
Father Junipero Serra personally founded nine California missions, three of these in Southern California: San Diego, San Juan Capistrano and San Buenaventura (now more commonly thought of as Ventura). His successors established many more, including Santa Barbara and San Gabriel.

Capital City

The city of Sacramento, which was founded in 1849 and is the oldest incorporated city in California, is also the state capital. Population-wise, Sacramento, with its roughly 407,000 residents, is the seventh largest city in the state.

Why San Diego Isn't Called San Miguel

It was the bay, not the city, that was actually named first. Juan Rodriguez Cabrillo dubbed it San Miguel Bay when he arrived there in 1542. Sixty years later, when Sebastian Vizcaino sailed up the coast, he entered the bay and promptly named it San Diego de Alcala—despite the fact that he had been given firm orders not to rename anything that the beloved Cabrillo had named already. The Franciscan monks established Mission San Diego de Alcala there in 1769, the first of 21 California missions. San Diego was not formally incorporated as a city until 1885.

El Pueblo de Nuestra Senora la Reina de Los Angeles del Rio de Porciuncula

Or, the City of Our Lady the Queen of the Angels on the River Porciuncula, better known to the world as Los Angeles, or simply L.A. As a pueblo, its function was to supply food to the soldiers of the Presidio, who were there to protect the missions. Los Angeles had one small problem, though. Hard as it is to believe today, no one wanted to live there! Captain Fernando Rivera was supposed to bring 24 married settlers and 34 married soldiers. But even the enticement of free land and supplies brought in only 11 families. Although San José lays claim to being the first California city established (1777), Los Angeles is a close second (1781).

Brigham's San Bernadino

The city of San Bernardino began from land purchased by the Mormons in 1851 from Rancho San Bernardino, a Mexican land grant awarded to Antonio Maria Lugo to graze cattle. The city was meant to be the first in a string of cities that would link Salt Lake City to the port of San Pedro. But after only a few short years, Brigham Young called the settlers all back to Salt Lake City, and two-thirds of them went, despite having just built an infrastructure of roads, housing, irrigation and sawmills.

The Family Farm

Horace and Daeida Wilcox originally came to Cahuenga Valley, a part of the Rancho La Brea land grant, to farm. But in 1887, Horace realized he could do a lot better by turning the family farm into a subdivision and selling lots for $150 an acre. Luckily for the Wilcoxes, their idea coincided with the arrival of the fledgling movie industry. Oh, the name of that little subdivision? Hollywood.

Anything for a Buck

Santa Clarita is a new town (incorporated in 1987) that is actually the result of the merger of some older ones—Saugus, Valencia, Canyon County, Newhall and some of Castaic. Apparently this was done, at least in part, to keep tax dollars local.

Not in Their Backyard

The City of West Covina was incorporated in 1923, when 507 residents banded together to prevent the City of Covina from establishing a sewage farm within the present city's boundaries.

Ah, Those Crafty Duck Hunters

Fullerton owes its existence to two brothers from back east, George and Edward Amerige. While on a duck hunting trip in the region, they heard rumors that California Central Railroad was planning to build a rail line through the area, and they quickly acted to purchase land for a town. Then they worked out a deal with a railroad executive named George Fullerton, negotiating with him until he changed the rail line so that it ran right through their new town. Do you think he got a little more out of the deal than just having a town named after him?

Good Decision
Buena Park was founded by James Whitaker, a wholesale grocer from Chicago. He bought some land from the former Rancho Los Coyotes in 1885, thinking he'd start a cattle ranch, but some officials from the Santa Fe Railroad managed to persuade him that he should start a town instead.

Bass-Ackwards?

Garden Grove owes its existence to Alonzo Cook, an attorney and physician who came to a small farming community and, six years later, left it with land for its first school and post office. Some people found his choice of a name odd, as the area didn't look like much of a garden. Cook responded by telling people to plant trees so that it would live up to its name.

Maybe Not the Best Name for a Dry Town
Riverside was founded in 1870 by John North, a pro-temperance abolitionist from Tennessee. He envisioned a place that would attract people more interested in culture than saloons. In letters and pamplets, he encouraged easterners to come west to this healthful place, believing that the colony would eventually be 10,000 people strong. That's a lot of teetotalers.

Ego Does Sometimes Enter the Equation

Downey was founded by and named after John Gately Downey, a former California governor, in 1870.

A TRIVIA TIMELINE

Red Letter Dates in
Southern California History

☛ Juan Rodriguez Cabrillo and crew leave the west coast of New Spain (now Mexico), arriving in what will come to be known as San Diego Bay in 1542.

☛ Father Junipero Serra embarks on his Alta California mission building for Spain by founding Mission San Diego de Alcala in 1769.

☛ After a long and bloody war, Mexico declares independence from Spain in 1821, and Alta California becomes Mexican territory.

☛ The United States declares war on Mexico in 1846. Fighting in California ends in 1847 with the surrender of Andres Pico to John C. Fremont, and the larger Mexican-American War comes to an end with the Treaty of Guadalupe Hidalgo in 1848.

☛ California is admitted as the 31st state of the Union on September 9, 1850.

☛ The Transcontinental Railroad is completed on May 10, 1869, finally linking relatively inaccessible California to the rest of the country. The Southern Pacific Railroad, the first transcontinental railroad to reach Los Angeles, arrives in 1876.

☛ The dawn of the citrus industry arrives inconspicuously in 1873, when Eliza Tibbets of Riverside is given three branches of an orange tree from Brazil. This was how the naval orange came to California.

☛ The first Los Angeles Aqueduct is completed in 1913, transporting, or some might say stealing, water from the Owens Valley, ensuring that the city's expanding need for water is met.

☛ In 1910, D.W. Griffith and his production company are sent to California, and they start filming on a vacant lot near Georgia Street in downtown Los Angeles. The first film ever shot in Hollywood proper is called *In Old California*. It is a story about Mexican California of the 1800s. Griffith returns to New York and reports favorably about California, and in 1913, many filmmakers head west, in part to escape Thomas Edison's monopoly on film patents.

☛ Los Angeles hosts the Summer Olympics in 1932. The Olympic Village constructed for the male athletes served as the prototype of many Olympic Villages to come.

☛ On August 11, 1965, the Watts Riot explodes when a white California Highway Patrolman named Lee Mininkus pulls over an African-American driver named Marquette Frye. Although on the surface this was a routine procedure, it became the catalyst for the pent-up anger of the 99-percent African-American population of the area, who were fed up with what they perceived to be racially motivated police brutality. By the end of the riots 144 hours later, there were 34 people dead, 1032 reported injuries and an estimated loss of property of over $40 million.

☛ The Olympics return to Los Angeles in 1984.

☛ Riots once again devastate Los Angeles when, on April 29, 1992, four police officers are acquitted of the beating of Rodney King, despite having been videotaped doing it. The riots left at least 53 people dead and caused $800 million in damage.

Oil was discovered in the state in 1892. By 1923, Los Angeles was supplying one-quarter of the world's petroleum needs.

THE "HOW" OR "WHY" BEHIND PLACE NAMES

Veneration of the Saints

All California communities with names beginning with San or Santa are named after saints of the Catholic Church. Typically, a town would be named after the saint whose feast day conincided with the day of the town's founding. San Juan Capistrano, Santa Monica, Santa Barbara and San Fernando del Rey are but a few.

Home Sweet Heim

Anaheim was founded by German immigrants, who combined the name "Ana," from the nearby Santa Ana River, with *heim*, which is German for "home."

Well it Wasn't Based on the Native Vegetation, That's for Sure

One story of the origin of the name "Hollywood" has it that the name originally belonged to someone's eastern summer home.

The wife of a developer asked to use it as the name of the new community they were building.

Delusions of Grandeur?

Many residents of La Jolla believe its name comes from the Spanish word for "jewel." In fact, it's just as likely to have come from a northern Mexican word meaning "a hollow in a seashore or river."

O Canada

The name "Ontario" might seem a little out of place in these parts. It's no surprise, then, that it's a Canadian import. The community was named by two engineering brothers, George and William Chaffey, after their native province.

The Other Burbank

You might guess with some confidence that Burbank was named after the famous horticulturist Luther Burbank, who once lived in Santa Rosa. It is actually named for David Burbank, a dentist and industrialist who was yet another of those savvy railroad speculators of which Southern Californian history seems to be full. He bought land from two of the old ranchos and began a successful sheep ranch there. Eventually, though, he sold the right of way through the land to Southern Pacific Railroad for one dollar. In 1886, a group of land speculators purchased much of his land for $250,000. They built a city and named it for the man they must have thanked their lucky stars for.

If You Name It, They Will Come

Pomona, established in 1875, was named by town boosters after the Roman goddess of fruit, even though, at that time, not a single orange tree had been planted there. Talk about unbounded optimism. Within the decade, Pomona had both the rail ties and the water to make it a hub of the citrus-growing industry.

Back to Our Pseudo-Spanish Roots

Harper was named after a neighborhood rancher. But in 1920, the town decided to reinvent itself as Costa Mesa, which means "coastal table."

All Dairy, All the Time

Three cities originally paid tribute to cows, or more specifically the dairies that profited from cows, when they incorporated. La Palma was originally called Dairyland, which didn't work so well once all the dairies had relocated. Although Cypress was originally nicknamed Waterville because of a large number of artesian wells, it also wanted a reference to dairy in its name when it incorporated, and called itself Dairy City. And Cerritos was incorporated in 1956 as Dairy Valley. All three towns were centers of the dairy industry, but as property became more valuable, prices pushed the dairies out, and the towns had some incentive to change their names.

As Translated from the Chumash

We know it today as Malibu, but the native peoples called the area *Humaliwo*, which means, "the waves crash loudly."

Simi Valley was also inhabited by the Chumash, and according to some people, "Simi" comes from their word *shimiji*, meaning "little white clouds." (I wonder what the Chumash term would be for "retired white policemen," a significant portion of the Simi Valley population today?)

Castaic is also thought to come from a Native American word, *kashtuk*, meaning "eyes."

The names of the towns of Piru and nearby Lake Piru are both derived from a Chumash word meaning "reeds."

How German Is It?

Ojai is the Chumash word for "nest." But when this small Ventura County city was founded in 1874, it was actually called Nordhoff. It was renamed Ojai when, in the political climate after World War I, Nordhoff was thought to be too German-sounding.

From the Tongvan and Tataviam

Pacoima comes from the Tataviam word for "entrance."

The name "Topanga," as in Topanga Canyon, derives from a Tongvan word and means "a place above."

The word *cahuenga*, as in Cahuenga Pass, comes from the name of a Tongvan village and means "place of the mountain."

Rancho Cucamonga bears traces of both its Native American and Spanish past in its name. The most likely translation of Cucamonga is "sandy place."

DID YOU KNOW?

Lots of towns begin with the word *rancho*, which reveals that they were once part of a Mexican or Spanish land grant. Even an Anglo-sounding town such as South Gate shares this legacy. It was once part of Rancho San Antonio and started as a cluster of homes, factories and commercial sites that grew up at the south end of this once vast holding.

EVERY TOWN HAS A STORY

Lord Help the Sister who Comes Between Me and My...Other Sister

On May 30, 2006, Irvine signed a sister-city memorandum with the Xuhui district of Shanghai, which disavowed the legitimacy of Taiwan's sovereignty. This agreement barred Irvine officials from visiting their previous sister city in Taoyuan, Taiwan.

There are just a couple of small problems, however. Irvine is not legally allowed to enter into international agreements that are counter to U.S. foreign policy. Also, it just so happens that roughly 10,000 American people of Taiwanese descent live in Irvine, and they were none too happy about this decision. About 200 demonstrators came to the Irvine council meeting and demanded that the agreement be voided. So the city drafted a new version of the memorandum, leaving out that whole pesky issue of Taiwanese sovereignty.

It's Not About the Waves, It's About the Branding

Huntington Beach *is* Surf City, U.S.A. Or so say the trademark rights to the name it was granted in May 2006. Santa Cruz, located farther north along the Central Coast, wasn't happy about this, because its citizens considered it to be the real Surf City. In fact, then mayor of Santa Cruz, Mike Rotkin, even wrote a song about it that challenged Huntington Beach to a surf-off for the title.

It's Not About the Waves, It's About the Sand

Every July, Imperial Beach holds the U.S. Sandcastle Open. It currently draws 350,000 visitors for the weekend to witness the creations of sandcastle makers from all over the United States. The top prize winner earns $5000, which is no small change considering the art will be completely washed away by the next incoming tide.

It's Not About the Waves, It's About the…Whale?

Lynne Cox, the long distance swimmer famed for setting a record for swimming over a mile in the freezing waters of Antarctica, was just 17 years old when, taking a morning swim off Seal Beach, she encountered a lost and stranded baby whale. Make that an 18-foot-long baby whale, in case you were thinking of it as a cute little cuddly thing. After getting over her initial shock and fear, she determined to not only save it from beaching itself and dying, but also to try to return it to its mother. She recorded that experience in her 2006 book, *Grayson*, which was what she called the little fella. Uh, maybe better make that *big* fella.

ANNUAL COMMUNITY EVENTS

Hold that Pose

In addition to being an acclaimed art festival, Laguna Beach's Festival of Arts is also a unique one. Every night of the festival, the Pageant of the Masters is held, which is a 90-minute, "living pictures" show in which famous art works, both classical and contemporary, are recreated by live actors. The pageant has come a long way from its humble beginnings in 1932, when struggling Laguna Beach officials hoped to mitigate the effects of the Great Depression by luring folks attending the Olympic Games in Los Angeles out their way with a town-sized art festival. A particular success came from the inspiration of former vaudevillian Lolita Perine, who dressed her fellow citizens in costumes and posed them behind a simple picture frame in the first pageant. These days there's an outdoor amphitheater, an orchestra, a narrator and professional lights and staging.

Agitprop, 19th-Century Style

The small town of Hemet, in the region south of the San Bernardino Mountains, stages an annual dramatic re-enactment of Helen Hunt Jackson's enormously popular, 19th-century novel *Ramona*. The novel, consciously imitating Jackson's friend Harriet Beecher Stowe's *Uncle Tom's Cabin*, called attention to the grievous plight of the Mission Indians of California, whom she had come to know on her travels. But of course, what American readers ate up was the story of forbidden love between a mixed-race girl and an Indian boy, and the romanticized vision of California's Spanish past. Hemet has been re-enacting the drama since 1923 in a natural outdoor theater called, suitably enough, the Ramona Bowl. The pageant features a 400-member cast, made up largely of residents. It is thought to be the largest and longest running play in the U.S., and it is the official outdoor play of California. It's hard to say, though, if Helen Hunt Jackson would be satisfied that she'd gotten her point across.

A Fabulous Festival of Flowers

The Tournament of Roses Parade was started by the Valley Hunt Club, many of whose members hailed from colder climes back east. They decided to revel a little in their mild winters by holding a rose parade while most of the country was still buried under snow. The floats were originally horse-drawn carriages covered in flowers. Over the next few years, motorized floats and the all-important marching bands were added.

The Tournament of Roses Parade was first held in Pasadena on January 1, 1890, and it has been held every year since. The parade has followed the same route for decades. It takes the floats about two and a half hours to complete the 5.5-mile route. From 1923 until recent years, it has been held in conjunction with the Rose Bowl, but in 2002 and 2006, the game was not held on the same day as the parade because it was also the BCS (Bowl Championship Series) National Championship Game, the championship title game, which rotated between the four college bowls in the series.

For about two days after the parade, the floats are left on display in "float barns" in Victory Park so that visitors can see them up close. Because of the work that it takes to complete a float, any on display are definitely worth taking a look at. Originally, floats were built by volunteers, but nowadays most have been built by professional float-building companies.

Even though much else has changed over the years, all of the floats still use real, fresh flowers. A good estimate is that it takes 10 people 10 hours for 10 days to decorate a float. It's a very labor-intensive craft. Some of the more delicate flowers must be put in their own separate vials of water and then attached to the float one by one. The number of flowers used in a single float is more than what a typical florist will use in five years. Luckily, the float's sponsor pays for all the flowers.

Each year, a theme is decided upon well in advance. Recent themes have included Celebration 2000: Visions of the Future; Music, Music, Music; and It's Magical. The theme for 2008 is Passport to the World's Celebrations. That should give the float designers a lot of scope.

Also every year, a Queen of the Tournament is selected out of about 1000 Pasadena girls who apply. The six princesses and one queen ride a float in the parade and, of course, spend a lot of time as parade promoters during their free hours.

Seems Like a Long Time to Wait for a Date

It only makes sense that, being situated in the California desert, settlers to Indio would consider date palms an interesting and likely lucrative crop. The first trees were transplanted to the area from Algeria in 1903, and by 1920, the crop had become a major producer. And because everyone loves a fair, celebrating the annual date harvest was as good a reason as any to host one. In 1921, the first Date Festival was held, but 16 years would lapse after the second annual event before the idea was resurrected as the Riverside County Fair and Coachella Valley Date Festival, bringing in 5000 fairgoers who took advantage of the 72 booths and exhibits. Over the years, the fair continued to grow. When World War II ended, an "Arabian Nights" theme was added, with events such as emu and ostrich races. The fair is held in February.

Floyd Shields and his wife Bess, owners and operators of Shields Date Gardens since 1924, not only ran a successful date-growing business, but Floyd also did quite a bit of research into the famed fruit. To that end, he produced a 15-minute documentary called *Romance and Sex Life of the Date.* For a free showing, just stop by Shields Date Gardens Inc. store on U.S. Highway 111, Indio. The show plays all day long—talk about endurance!

Holy Hot Rods!

Every July, thousands turn out at Hansen Dam Park in Los Angeles County for the annual Blessing of the Cars, an event started by Stephanie and Gabriel Baltierra. Gabriel, coming from the Catholic tradition, had seen many things blessed over time, but perhaps nothing he loved so much as his car. He and his wife, Stephanie, who shared the car love enough to belong to an all female car club called The Minxes, invited a few hundred close friends to have a morning mass, then have their cars blessed by the Catholic priest, who went from car to car, sometimes putting holy water in the radiator. The hundreds became thousands, and these days the event is an all-day and into-the-night affair. Stephanie says that some people have claimed that the event attracts "more tattoos than the Navy," but says that the real common denominator is that everyone there is just passionate about their cars.

There's Gold in Them Thar Hills...
Somewhere

If you're ever in Borrego Springs on April Fool's Day, you might do worse than to see how you fare in the annual Peg Leg Smith Liar's Contest. First you have to find it, though. It's held at the Peg Leg Smith Monument, about seven miles down a two-lane highway outside the city. Peg Leg, a.k.a. Thomas L. Smith, was a 19th-century mountain man and prospector who liked to spin tall tales. He claimed to have located a gold mine worth a fortune in these parts—it was just that he had forgotten exactly where it was. In the Liar's Contest, entrants must tell a five-minute tale about Peg Leg—the taller, the better. The winner gets what you might call a recycled trophy, donated for the occasion. As the contestants say, when you get it home, you can lie about what you got it for.

COMMUNITIES' CLAIMS TO FAME

Playground of the Stars

Palm Springs had its heyday from the 1930s to the 1950s, when the Hollywood A-list flocked to see and be seen in its night-clubs, hotels and restaurants. Thanks to this era, Palm Springs has the highest concentration of mid-20th-century modern architecture in the United States and was recognized by the National Trust for Historic Preservation for its efforts to pre-serve mid-century architecture. After World War II, many renowned architects gravitated towards Palm Springs. Inspired by the Bauhaus aesthetic, they found a resonance in the desert, and Desert Modernism was born. Some of the landmarks of Palm Springs architecture include Albert Frey's Tramway Gas Station, Donald Wexler's airport, Stuart William's Coachella Savings and Loan, Richard Neutra's Kaufmann House and Palmer and Krisel's House of Tomorrow.

A Little Bit of Italy

The tobacco millionaire Abbott Kinney took a look at the marshy dunes south of Santa Monica and saw something there that most people wouldn't have—a Venice of America. To drain the area, several miles of canals were dug, first by men and animals and then, when it proved too much for them, by steam machines. Tourists were drawn by the canals, as well as a 1200-foot pier, a hot saltwater plunge and an arcade with Venetian architecture. But Kinney failed to foresee one thing—the rapid advance of the automobile. Over the protest of the locals, the city filled in half the canals, which were difficult to maintain, to fulfill the demand for ever more roadways. After that, the region began to languish. But as real estate prices took off around this depressed region towards the end of the 20th century, the city of Los Angeles finally agreed in 1994 to refurbish the six remaining canals at a cost of $6 million. Here is some more Venice trivia:

☛ Venice was the birthplace of the rock band The Doors. Before they made their fortune, the band often played in local Venice clubs.

☛ Venice is the home of Ince Field, the first official airport in California. It was located near the intersection of Washington and Venice Boulevards. Because of surrounding development, the airport was unable to expand, and homes and stores were built on it in 1923.

☛ In 1926, Aimee Semple MacPherson, the most famous evangelist of her day, disappeared in the waters near her Venice hotel. People searched by air and by water for her, and one lifeguard drowned in the search. But a few days after her memorial service, she reappeared, saying that she had been kidnapped. Although various charges were brought against her for offenses such as fabricating evidence and corruption of morals, eventually they were all dropped.

☛ The 1970s were the era of the Linnie Canal Downwind Boat Race. On a secret Sunday afternoon in summer, contestants were given two hours to build their boats and sail them down the Linnie Canal. Masts had to be lowered to get past the three canal bridges.

Drive-by Shopping

The Miracle Mile is a stretch of Wilshire Boulevard between Fairfax and La Brea Avenues near downtown Los Angeles. It was originally developed by A.W. Ross in the 1920s, when he had a crucial insight into the era that lay ahead and understood that a shopping district would now have to meet the needs of a cruising automobile and not just those of pedestrians. He basically invented a new, car-oriented architectural model, which Reyner Banham called the "linear downtown," in which shop windows were bigger and closer to the road, signage was simplified so as to be seen at a faster pace and stores had to have space for parking lots behind them. It may seem obvious enough now, but that's just because his vision proved both so practical and so lucrative that it was quickly embraced as a model for shopping districts across the country.

Sticky, Gooey, Icky

One of the most fascinating sites in downtown L.A. isn't very urban at all. La Brea Tar Pits are located on Miracle Mile right down the street from Petersen Automotive Museum, and asphalt or tar seeps to the surface in a cluster of pits that have been around for tens of thousands of years. Over the course of such a vast stretch of time, many plants and animals have become trapped in the sticky tar and have sunk beneath the surface and become fossilized. Such prehistoric creatures as mammoths, ground sloths, dire wolves and saber-toothed cats have all been found there. There was even one excavation of human remains: a woman, perhaps Chumash, who had been bashed on the head approximately 9000 years ago.

The pits have been excavated since the beginning of the 20th century, and one pit, Pit 91, has been continuously excavated every summer from July through early September since 1969, making it the longest ongoing urban excavation of prehistoric life in the world. Although these days, scientists are more interested in microfossils than mammoths, the nearby George Page Museum has the whole range of fossils on exhibition. Since 1906, more than one million bones have been excavated from the tar pits.

Aviatrix-in-Training
Amelia Earhart learned to fly in South Gate, at an unpaved airstrip called Kinner Field.

The Greeter

For years, Laguna Beach has had an official welcoming party. Eiler Larsen, a Dane with hair falling below his shoulders and a big, gray beard, was affectionately known as "the greeter." He most commonly stood at the corner of Forest Avenue and the Pacific Coast Highway, waving to everyone who drove by. Eventually, the city council proclaimed Larsen the Official Greeter. Although he died in 1979, he is not forgotten. He is immortalized in two statues: one at Greeter's Restaurant and another in front of the Pottery Shack. The Greeter symbolizes the welcoming feeling that people sense when they come to Laguna Beach. It must be catching, because a new greeter, Mr. Number One Archer, has taken up Larsen's post since 1981. He says he is just carrying on the tradition.

Sand with Sizzle

From the 1930s to the 1950s, a section of Santa Monica Beach just south of the Santa Monica Pier became known as Muscle Beach. In the mid-1930s, a bunch of boys began to gather there to work out in the sand and perform gymnastic feats. By the late 1930s, there were 50 or 60 regular performers, and crowds of thousands came to watch them, especially on weekends. When World War II came, many of the regulars were commissioned by the City of Santa Monica to sell war bonds. One of their number, Jack Kornoff, appeared bare-chested and holding a rifle on the cover of *LOOK* magazine, apparently to represent the fitness of the American military man.

In the 1950s, complaints began to arise about Muscle Beach, which some local business people were beginning to find offensive. When tawdry headlines revealed that some of the weight lifters had been consorting with underage girls, Muscle Beach was shut down and bulldozed. The City claimed the beach had become a magnet for "perverts" and "narcissistic parasites." But in truth, Santa Monica had had a love-hate relationship with the beach all along.

Muscle Beach, the Sequel

In 1959, the original Muscle Beach was closed, and the City of Los Angeles Parks and Recreation Department opened a new Muscle Beach on the Venice Boardwalk, where it remains to this day. Soon thereafter the "Pit" came into being, and some new bodybuilding legends came into prominence, such as Arnold Schwarzenegger, Franco Columbo and Dave Draper.

 There were some famous names to come out of the original Muscle Beach, too. Vic Tanney, Joe Gold and Jack La Lanne all built fitness empires out of their gymnastic skills. And Steve Reeves, who became famous in the title role of the movie *Hercules,* was one of several stuntmen who got their start there.

Have We Been Here Before?

The Owens Valley is not only renowned for being a contender in the vicious water wars of an earlier era, but it also contains the Alabama Hills, which may be one of the most familiar sites in the world even if, like most of us, you've never been there. Its odd-looking rock formation proved to be a useful backdrop for a variety of settings. Since the 1920s, it has been a shooting site for 150 movies, including *Gunga Din* and *How the West Was Won*, and numerous TV shows, especially westerns such as *The Lone Ranger* and *Hopalong Cassidy.*

ALL THINGS HOLLYWOOD

The Early Days

☞ Until 1900, there were hundreds of camels in the Hollywood Hills. These were a remnant of the U.S. Army's brief experiment with a Camel Corps back in 1856. As a result of the Civil War, the Camel Corps was disbanded in 1862, and the camels were set free.

☞ The first motion picture studio, the Nestor Film Company, a transplant from New Jersey, opened in 1911.

☞ Early actors rehearsed scenes to a stopwatch because sentences had to be perfectly timed to the number of feet of film available.

☞ Some early movie studios operated out of barns. Horses and cows were cast as extras.

Maybe the Biggest Star

There's no more famous landmark of Southern California than the Hollywood sign. Here is all you need to know about it (and probably a little more).

☞ In 1923, the Hollywood sign was born. Real estate promoters spent $21,000 to erect a sign on Mt. Cahuenga advertising some property in the hills. The sign read "Hollywoodland."

☞ Each of the original 13 letters was 30 feet wide and 50 feet tall. There was also a dot, 35 feet in diameter, with lights around the perimeter, which was below the sign and was intended to catch people's eyes.

- The sign had 4000 20-watt bulbs spaced eight inches apart. Different parts of the sign flashed at night. It could be seen without mechanical aid from 25 miles away.

- In September 1932, Peg Entwistle, an acclaimed East Coast stage actress who was unable to make it in Hollywood, climbed the letter "H" and leaped to her death.

- The developers who created the sign went bankrupt during the Depression.

- From 1939 until the end of World War II, maintenance of the sign stopped. Some 4000 light bulbs were stolen. Neighbors lobbied for the sign's removal.

- In 1944, the defunct developers sold off the last 450 acres of their property to the City of Los Angeles. This sale included the sign.

- In 1949, the Chamber of Commerce repaired the sign, removing the letters that spelled "land."

- In 1973, the Cultural Heritage Board of the City of Los Angeles gave the sign landmark status, declaring it Cultural-Historical Monument No. 111.

- The Hollywood Sign Trust got the big players on board to help with preservation. At a fundraiser at the Playboy Mansion, each letter was auctioned off for $28,000. Alice Cooper bought an "O," Gene Autry bought an "L" and Paul Williams bought the "W." As a result, a refurbished sign was unveiled in 1978. The Hollywood community, which had fallen on hard times, was symbolically reignited.

- In 1984, the Olympics came to L.A., and the sign was illuminated for two weeks in honor of the event.

- In 1992, Dan Lundgren, the attorney general of California, designated three bodies to safeguard the sign's preservation. The Hollywood Sign Trust became responsible for its protection, preservation and promotion; the Hollywood Chamber of Commerce is responsible for protecting its image and both approving and licensing its likeness; and the City of Los Angeles guarantees its security within Griffith Park.

☛ Dutch Boy Paints gave the sign a new paint job in 1995. Phyllis Diller presided over the unveiling, which was obscured by fog.

☛ A lightening bolt took out the sign's security system in one fell swoop, but the system was replaced by a much more advanced one.

☛ Digital surveillance was added in 1999.

☛ The sign was lit as a focal point for ushering in the new millennium. The letters were illuminated one by one, and Jay Leno presided over the light show that followed, which was fueled by over two million watts of energy.

☛ The sign was refurbished in 2005, requiring Ceryllium advanced coating and weeks of prep work and painting, which was particularly challenging on the steep hillside. L.A. mayor Antonio Villaraigosa actually repelled down the slope to add the last strokes of coating.

☛ Security is tighter than ever now that the Hollywood Sign Trust has teamed up with Homeland Security to upgrade its surveillance system.

☛ It will probably come as no surprise to most readers that there is a 24-hour webcam at the sign, and that you can look at the city through it 24/7. But did you know that you can also view the sign from space? If you have Quicktime, you can see it from a celestial viewpoint right from your computer.

DID YOU KNOW?

Prankster Danny Finegood altered the sign on several occasions. On January 1, 1976, he used fabric to make the sign read "Hollyweed," to celebrate some liberal marijuana laws coming into effect in California. That same year, he made the sign read "Holywood" for Easter. He even managed to make the sign read "Oil War" in protest to the first Gulf War. Unfortunately, park rangers removed the sheeting before sunrise. Danny was only 52 years old when he died on January 22, 2007, and some of his best pranks may have still been ahead of him. But perhaps not. Homeland Security has become pretty vigilant, and maybe it just wasn't fun anymore for Danny.

Star-Studded Street

The Hollywood Walk of Fame is the closest most of us will ever get to actually touching a celebrity, so to speak. The idea originated in 1958 when artist Oliver Weismuller was hired to come up with an idea to breathe new life into the city. Representatives are chosen for one of five categories: film, television, recording, broadcast and theater, and each is differentiated from the others by its own, unique icon. Joanne Woodward was the first celebrity to be honored, receiving a star on February 9, 1960. Since then, more than 2300 of the original 2500 stars created have been assigned and laid out along Hollywood Boulevard.

Conjurer's Castle

The Magic Castle is a private clubhouse in Hollywood for a group called Magical Arts, Inc., which centers its mission around encouraging and promoting the public's interest in magic, with a special emphasis on the history and tradition of the magic arts. Entrance is available only to members or members' guests. You don't have to be a magician to get an associate's membership, but a Magical Arts member must be versed in the history of magic and be able to perform a few simple magic tricks.

The building, built in 1908, lies in the hills above Hollywood. The first illusion is perhaps its size, because it's reputed to be much bigger inside than it appears from the outside. Many celebrity magicians have been inside, including Cary Grant, Johnny Carson and Steve Martin. The most recent was Jason Alexander, better known to many as George Costanza, of *Seinfeld* fame.

Where the Stars Leave Their Mark

Grauman's Chinese Theatre opened in 1927 with the world premiere of Cecil B. DeMille's silent film *King of Kings*. The theater's Chinese Baroque style, with a dragon winding it's way across the front, stone lion-dogs at the entrance and miniature dragons swirling around its copper roof, makes it one of the great theaters of the world in its own right. Apart from being the site of many world premieres to this day, and of having hosted the Academy Awards in the 1940s, its real claim to fame is its famous forecourt, where close to 200 stars have left their signatures, handprints and footprints. Facts about the forecourt

could probably fill up a small trivia book on their own, but here are some of the highlights:

☛ The first stars to be immortalized in cement were Douglas Fairbanks, Mary Pickford and Norma Talmadge when the theater opened in 1927—understandable, since both Fairbanks and Pickford had a financial stake in the theater.

☛ The smallest adult footprints are those of Jeannette MacDonald at 6.5 inches in length. Of course, they can't really compete with the bare footprint Shirley Temple left when she was a child.

☛ Three horses have immortalized their hoofprints alongside their master's more conventional ones: Roy Rogers' Trigger, Tom Mix's Tony and Gene Autry's Champion.

☛ Groucho Marx left the imprint of his cigar, Al Jolsen of his knees and Jimmy Durante of his famous "schnozolla," while R2D2, the robot of *Star Wars* fame, left an imprint of its tread marks.

☛ Harpo Marx and Sean Connery were the only adults not to wear shoes for their footprints. Harpo also left a sketch of his harp in the cement.

☛ Ventriloquist Edgar Bergan drew a quick caricature of his famous sidekick, Charlie McCarthy.

☛ Marilyn Monroe dotted the "i" in her name with a rhinestone, but it was later chipped out by a committed memento seeker.

The forecourt has few blank paving stones left, and Hollywood legends are still being asked to get down and dirty for immortality's sake. But if you're planning on being commemorated as a Hollywood superstar, you'd better hurry up with that game plan. Time's a-wasting.

TO ERR IS HUMAN— COMMUNITY DISASTERS

In Their Blind Spot

On September 25, 1978, Pacific Southwest Airlines Flight 182 from Los Angeles was on its final approach into San Diego's Lindbergh Field when it crashed into a private Cessna 172. A total of 144 people were killed, including all passengers on both flights as well as seven people on the ground, making it the worst California aircraft disaster to date (and let's hope ever). The conclusion of the National Transportation Safety Board was that the PSA flight crew had failed to fully follow air traffic control procedures, in that they had lost sight of the smaller plane, which was directly beneath them, and had not notified air traffic control.

After the disaster, which also left nine others on the ground injured as well as 22 homes damaged or destroyed, a local controversy was revived about why such a busy airfield was located in such a densely populated area. But despite proposals for alternate sites, San Diego International Airport remains in place— the busiest single runway airport in the world.

A Dam Shame

The St. Francis Dam was built in 1924–26 to create a reservoir near the community of Santa Clarita for William Mulholland's Los Angeles Aqueduct. Three minutes before midnight on March 12, 1928, the dam failed, and the resulting flood killed more than 600 people. It was the worst civil engineering failure of the 20th century, and the disaster is second only to the 1906 San Francisco earthquake in terms of loss of life in California history. The dam failure also ended the career of William Mulholland, who had seen the cracks and leaks in the dam in the years before and had been notified of them even closer to the night of the disaster, but he had ignored them. To his credit, he took all responsibility for the disaster upon himself. However, a jury, though finding fault with some of his practices, ultimately cleared Mulholland of any criminal charges. During the course of the investigation, it was discovered that the dam had been built against an ancient undetected landslide. The geologists who had originally surveyed the land had not known how unstable the rock formations around the dam were, and Mulholland could not have known either.

Runaway Train!

On June 21, 2003, a series of freight cars carrying lumber broke loose during a switching operation and rolled 27 miles down the tracks with no engine and no one on board before officials decided to use a remote system to switch the cars to side tracks. Although they knew this meant the train would very likely derail somewhere, they wanted to prevent a derailment from happening in heavily populated downtown Los Angeles. Unfortunately for some people near the tracks in Commerce City, 18 of the train's 30 cars derailed in their neighborhood, destroying two homes and rendering others inhabitable. Although 13 people were injured, miraculously none of these injuries was serious, and there were no deaths.

SURFING, SKATING, SEEKING—LIFE, CALIFORNIA-STYLE

Time and Tide Wait for No Dude

Although surfers have a reputation for being laid back, there is a fanatical component to their lifestyle all the same. The constantly changing conditions of ocean weather and tides make a devoted surfer a virtual slave to the sea.

Surf culture first began to be popularized in California in the 1960s and immediately required accoutrement, such as the classic "woodie" (a car with wood siding that was at that point out of fashion and therefore cheap), bikinis and board shorts and, of course, surf music. Surfer slang, including such phrases as "Gnarly, dude," and "Totally tubular," have long since permeated popular culture.

There are two surf museums along the Southern California coast. The International Surf Museum in Huntington Beach honors famous surfers, as well as those people who have made contributions to surf culture. Particularly revered is Duke Kahanamoku, who has his own statue. He's credited with pretty much single-handedly popularizing surfing on the world stage when he traveled with his redwood board after his swimming success in the 1912 and 1920 Olympics. There is plenty of other surfing memorabilia at the museum, including a heck of a lot of surfboards.

The second museum is the California Surf Museum in Oceanside. It has the first surfing trophy, which was named after Tom Blake, the first waterproof camera used to capture close-up footage and an exhibit on the history of surfboard shaping.

Zose Zenzational Z-Boys

Skateboard culture seemed to have emerged straight out of the surf culture around Pacific Ocean Park, the story of which was documented in the movie *Dogtown and Z-Boys*. Skateboarding already existed when the Zephyr Team came on the scene, but it would never be the same again after the team changed the rules at the 1975 championship in Del Mar, where they showed everyone else what they had learned skating the rims of asphalt parks and the walls of abandoned swimming pools.

His Crazy Life

Gang culture is another important subculture of Southern California. In his memoir *Always Running: La Vida Loca: Gang Days in L.A.*, Luis Rodriguez wrote about his days growing up in the gangs of East L.A. during the 1960s and '70s in hopes of helping his own son stay out of the gangs. Yet even today, gang culture remains a pervasive and seductive aspect of California culture. Gangs that originated in Los Angeles and Southern California, such as the Crips and the Bloods, have ended up with national name recognition because of their media exposure.

Peaceful, Prayerful Places

Another prominent California lifestyle is that of the seeker of enlightenment, particularly esoteric knowledge from the Far East. The Self-Realization Fellowship Lake Shrine, tucked away in the Pacific Palisades, is an excellent example. Surrounding a beautiful lake full of swans, ducks, koi and lotus flowers are a windmill that is actually a temple, a houseboat where Yogananda once stayed, a court of religions honoring the five principal religions of the world and the Mahatma Gandhi Peace Memorial, where a portion of Gandhi's ashes are buried. The weekly prayer services address such questions as the way to mental freedom, the eternal blessings of a true guru and the deeper teachings of Jesus Christ.

The Transcendental Meditation movement of Maharishi Mahesh Yogi had a university in Santa Barbara, although it eventually moved to Fairfield, Iowa.

Jiddu Krishnamurti, the famous spiritual teacher, lived in Ojai for many years, and today Ojai is the home of the Krishnamurti Foundation of America. Krishnamurti originally hung out with the theosophists, and it is no accident that the Krotona Institute for theosophy is also located in Ojai.

DRUGS, BOOZE AND ALL THINGS NAUGHTY

Teetotaling Teens They're Not

Although the rate of underage drinking remained about the same between 2002 and 2004 nationwide, it rose 15.8 percent among the 12- to 17-year-old crowd in California. In the same period, the number of these young people who said they'd used an illicit drug in the past month rose from 11.4 percent to 12.1 percent, despite a nationwide decline over the same period. Marijuana use was also up in this group during the period, from 14.1 percent to 14.6 percent. Only cocaine use was down, from 1.7 percent to 1.6 percent. Eight percent of the age group said they had used pain-relievers for non-medical purposes. And nine percent said that they abused or were dependent on drugs or alcohol to some degree, up from eight percent in 2002.

Don't Ask Me How I Know this Stuff

Sepulveda Boulevard between Roscoe Boulevard and Ventura Boulevard has been a street walking zone and drug addict's seamy paradise forever, despite sporadic attempts to clean it up. One undercover cop who has worked both Hollywood and this section of the Valley says that the big difference is that on Sepulveda, you don't have to bother to look enticing because the johns are on Sepulveda specifically for sex. A prostitute just shows up for work in a sweatshirt and jeans and fits right in.

SEXUAL PREFERENCE

West Hollywood

In less tolerant times, gay bars, along with casinos and other establishments that did not find favor with the powers that be, ran less risk of being raided by the Los Angeles Police Department if they were outside the city limits in the unincorporated county area of West Hollywood. In due course, an active gay and lesbian community began to settle there, and by 1983, citizens voted to incorporate as the City of West Hollywood. It is currently one of the most gay-friendly areas in the country, and its spirit of tolerance has attracted many artists, actors and designers of all persuasions.

Rise and Fall, West Hollywood–Style

In 1984, West Hollywood elected Valerie Terrigno, the first openly lesbian mayor of a major city. One of her first acts in that role was to remove a sign at the trendy Barney's Beanery that said "No Fags Allowed." Sadly, her luster tarnished a little when she was convicted of embezzling public funds in 1986. She was sentenced to 60 days for fraud and, at that point, stepped down from the city council.

Paying it Forward

West Hollywood can claim a couple of other firsts. It elected the first openly gay majority city council in the country in 1984, and as an example of how its atmosphere of tolerance has helped it embrace other concerns, in 1985 it tipped its hat to its large Russian Jewish constituency by being the first city in the United States to declare Yom Kippur an official holiday.

When You Can't Go Home Again

Strangely enough, San Diego's gay scene can be attributed at least in part to what's usually thought of as a conservative presence—that of the U.S. Military. After World War II, thousands of men and women who had discovered their sexual identity while in the armed services couldn't easily picture returning to the small, and perhaps small-minded, towns they had left behind, so they flocked to the port cities of San Diego and San Francisco that they had become familiar with during their term of service.

DID YOU KNOW?

According to the 2000 census, San Diego had a gay index of 186, which means that the city was 86 percent above the national norm in its proportion of same-sex, unmarried households within its general population. This gives it the highest gay index in Southern California, surpassing L.A.'s gay index of 168. Most of the gay population revolves around the hub community of Hillcrest, in Uptown San Diego.

In 2002, Superior Court Judge Bonnie Dumanis was elected San Diego District Attorney. She thus became the highest ranking openly lesbian law enforcement officer in the nation.

Opportunity Knocked

In 2005, city council member Toni Atkins became the acting mayor of San Diego when the mayor, Dick Murphy, resigned, and the deputy mayor, Michael Zucchet, was convicted on corruption charges, thus making San Diego the largest American city with an openly gay or lesbian chief executive.

Not Without its Risks

It hasn't always been a piece of cake to be "out" in conservative-minded San Diego. On July 24, 1999, hundreds of gay pride marchers and spectators were tear-gassed when an unidentified man threw a military-issue tear gas grenade into the Family Matters segment of the parade—which included small children, as if the act wasn't heinous enough already. The culprit was never found.

And at the 25th annual Gay Pride Parade, six men were assaulted while leaving the festivities at Balboa Park. Four suspects were arrested within a few days, and all pled guilty.

MONEY MATTERS

A Big Producer, and Not the Hollywood Kind

The GSP, or gross state product, was measured at about $1.62 trillion as of 2005, the largest in the country. California is in fact responsible for 13 percent of the United States' GDP, or gross domestic product, and just on its own is larger than all but eight countries in the world as far as GDP goes.

The (Very High) Cost of Living

☛ In Los Angeles, the overall cost of living is 48 percent higher than the national average. It is almost 20 percent higher in regard to health care.

☛ In San Diego, the overall cost of living is 52.1 percent higher than the national average, with health care costs at 30.3 percent above average.

☛ If you think that's bad, though, try making ends meet in Santa Barbara, where the overall cost of living is a whopping 129.7 percent higher than the national average and 113 percent higher for health care.

Little Boxes on the Hillside (but at this rate, they'll have to be cardboard boxes)

As of February 2007, Los Angeles County and Orange County top the list of least affordable urban markets *in the world*, at least as measured by median housing costs. The median house price was 11 times the median income in these two counties. San Diego trails right behind them at 10.5 times more, followed by Honolulu at 10.1, Ventura County at 9.4 and Stockton at 8.4.

And just to give some sense of what we're talking about when we say "median price," the median price for the Southland as a whole was $485,000 in January 2007.

TAXING SUBJECTS

Keeping the City Going

City sales tax for cities within Los Angeles County was almost universally 8.25 percent, the exception being Avalon at 8.75 percent. City sales tax in San Bernardino, San Diego, Orange and Riverside counties was slightly lower at 7.75 percent, the exceptions being 8.25 percent at El Cajon, Laguna Beach and South Laguna. Ventura County's sales tax lay still lower at 7.25 percent.

Why it Sometimes Makes Sense to Cross the City Line

Los Angeles City proper charges businesses a gross receipt tax, which is based on a percentage of business revenues, while neighboring areas charge only a small flat fee. So there are many communities that benefit from being near but not technically within the city limits of what many see as an "alpha world city."

After the City, the State Gets Its Chunk

The Franchise Tax Board is responsible for collecting California personal income tax and California business tax. Californians file more than 14 million state personal income tax returns, generating over $49.9 billion a year for the state. Businesses file more than one million returns each year, which brings in $10.4 billion annually. Despite what may sound like a pretty healthy revenue, the Franchise Tax Board claims that Californians as a whole owe about $6.5 billion in taxes more than they pay every year.

Those Revolting Property Owners

By far the most controversial taxation issue in recent California history was that which ended in the passage of Proposition 13 in 1978, officially named the People's Initiative to Limit Property Taxation, but also called the "Jarvis-Gann amendment" after Howard Jarvis and Paul Gann, the two men who spearheaded the tax revolt.

The passage of "Prop 13" put a cap on property tax rates, which in certain areas had been rising dramatically and were eating into the funds of people who were retired and on a fixed income. But tax reduction also ate into the budgets of state schools.

Proposition 13 set off a chain of such initiatives across the country and is believed to have been a major catalyst for conservative Ronald Reagan to win the presidential election in November 1980. On June 4, 1978, voters passed Prop 13 by 65 percent, with a 69 percent voter turnout. This was the highest off-year election turnout since 1916. (Off-year elections are rarely about electing anyone to national office and don't typically generate a lot of voter interest.)

DID YOU  KNOW?

The proposition came about because of California's initiative process, in which a proposed law or state constitutional amendment can be placed directly before voters, provided its supporters can get enough signatures on a petition before a prescribed date.

JOBS/NO JOBS

Working Hard or Hardly Working?

These employment figures were available for the years 2001–05 (the civilian labor force for California as a whole was 17,695,567 in 2005, and the unemployment rate was 5.4 percent):

Los Angeles County
Labor Force: 4,821,137 in 2005
Unemployment Rate: 5.3 percent in 2005
Total Jobs Lost Since 2001: 58,000 jobs; down 1.4 percent

Significant Job Gains:
• education and health care up 37,500 jobs (28,100 in health care and social assistance sector)
• leisure and hospitality up 28,900 jobs (24,700 in food services and drinking places)
• credit intermediation and related activities up 12,300 jobs

Significant Job Losses:
• manufacturing, information, professional and business services, government, agriculture, and natural resources and mining

Orange County
Labor Force: over 1.6 million in 2005; up 1.3 percent from 2004
Unemployment Rate: 3.4 percent in 2005
Total Jobs Gained Since 2001: 75,400 jobs; up five percent

Significant Job Gains:
• finance and insurance sector up 27,200 jobs
• health care and social assistance up 15,000 jobs
• construction up 18,600 jobs
• professional and business services up 18,600 jobs

Significant Job Losses:
• 25,800 jobs lost in manufacturing, particularly durable goods (19,800 jobs lost)

San Bernardino County

Labor Force: 863,400 in 2005; up 3.4 percent from 2001
Unemployment Rate: five percent in 2005
Total Jobs Gained Since 2001: 79,500 jobs; up 14 percent

Significant Job Gains:
- retail trade up 13,700 jobs
- employment services up 10,100 jobs
- construction up 9500 jobs (7600 with specialty trade contractors)

Significant Job Losses:
- information down 1400 jobs
- agriculture down 1200 jobs

Riverside County

Labor Force: 848,700 in 2005; up 19 percent from 2001
Unemployment Rate: 5.1 percent in 2005
Total Jobs Gained Since 2001: 105,200 jobs; up almost
  22 percent

Significant Job Gains:
- retail trade up 19,100 jobs
- construction up 24,200 jobs (specialty trade contractors up
  19,400)
- professional and business services up 15,000 jobs.
- government up 14,000 jobs (12,600 in local government)

There were no significant job losses.

Ventura County

Labor Force: 421,200 in 2005
Unemployment Rate: 4.7 percent in 2005
Total Jobs Gained Since 2001: 14,800 jobs; up almost five
  percent

Significant Job Gains:
- financial activities sector up 4800 jobs (4200 in credit media-
  tion and related activities)

- trade, transportation and utilities up 4000 jobs, all in the retail and wholesale trade component
- agriculture up 3200 jobs

There were no significant job losses.

San Diego County
Labor Force: over 1.5 million in 2005; up 1.1 percent from 2004
Unemployment Rate: 4.3 percent in 2005
Total Jobs Gained Since 2001: 62,700 jobs

Significant Job Gains:
- leisure and hospitality industry up 18,800 jobs, mainly in accommodation and food services
- construction up 16,300 jobs
- financial activities up 11,200 jobs (8400 in the finance and insurance sector)

Significant Job Losses:
- manufacturing down 14,800 jobs (10,600 in durable goods manufacturing)
- information industry down 1500 jobs
- agriculture down 700 jobs

Imperial County
Labor Force: 61,500 in 2005; up 10.6 percent from 2001
Unemployment Rate: 15.8 percent in 2005 (in part due to seasonal nature of agricultural work)
Total Jobs Gained Since 2001: 4100 jobs; up 8.2 percent

Significant Job Gains:
- retail trade up 1300 jobs
- non-durable goods manufacturing up 600 jobs

There were no significant job losses.

INDUSTRIOUS SOUTHERN CALIFORNIA

Apparently Southern California Ain't so Laid Back After All

Los Angeles County

In 2005, the leading industries of Los Angeles County were direct international trade, tourism, motion picture and TV production, technology, and business and professional services. As opposed to the "old" economy, which relied heavily on the aerospace industry and manufacturing jobs, the "new" economy of the county is technology driven and depends on access to the numerous technological research centers in the area. The leading sectors are bio-med technology, environmental technology and digital information technology.

Los Angeles is still the largest manufacturing center in the U.S., surprisingly enough, though its emphasis has shifted from highly paid aerospace workers to low-paid garment industry workers. In descending order, its chief products are apparel, computer and electronic products, transportation products, fabricated metal products, food products and furniture.

 The Los Angeles Customs District is the nation's busiest customs district, with more than 11 percent of all U.S. trade. In 2006, it set some records. It was the first customs district ever to surpass $300 billion in annual trade, and the first customs district to exceed $100 billion in annual trade with a single nation: China.

Orange County

Orange County's leading industries are tourism, technology, business and professional services, wholesale trade and logistics, and health services and bio-medicine. Orange County businesses are also very aggressive in international trade.

Technology has several clusters of activity in Orange County and centers around computer software, semi-conductors and bio-med applications. Orange County is another major manufacturing center, just behind Dallas and ahead of Atlanta. The biggest sectors are computer and electronic products, fabricated metal products, transportation products, textile mill products and apparel, and machinery.

San Bernardino County and Riverside County

The San Bernardino/Riverside area's leading industries are tourism, wholesale trade and logistics, health services and bio-medicine, agriculture and food products, manufacturing, and technology. This region, known as the Inland Empire, is growing as a manufacturing center in such areas as fabricated metal products, textile mills and apparel, transportation equipment, and plastics and rubber. Despite being inland, international trade does figure into the local economy because the area is a transportation hub for rail and truck service, and the area is also a major distribution center for companies moving goods from the ports to the rest of the U.S.

Ventura County

Ventura County's leading industries are agricultural and food products, tourism, technology, financial services, health services and bio-medicine.

Because of Port Hueneme, there's also an international trade component to Ventura County business. Port Hueneme is what's termed a "break-bulk" facility because it handles small, individually packaged units rather than bulk or container cargo. It handled 4,606,300 tons of cargo in 2005. The major commodities were cars, fruits and vegetables.

San Diego County

San Diego County's leading industries are tourism, technology, business and professional services, direct international trade and wholesale trade. The economy of San Diego County is often technology driven and includes bio-med, communication and computer science. San Diego is also a large manufacturing center, with computer and electronic products and transportation products leading the way.

International trade is a big component of the economy. The San Diego Customs District is a major channel for U.S./Mexican trade. In 2005, the total two-way trade through customs was $43.4 billion.

Tourism is another major industry for San Diego. Besides its own tourist attractions such as Seaworld and the San Diego Zoo, it also profits from travelers going to and from Mexico. Several cruise ships set sail from or make port calls at San Diego as well.

San Diego is home to major bio-tech industry headquarters, bio-tech research parks and several non-profit bio-tech groups as well, such as the Salk Institute for Biological Studies and the Scripps Institute. Major institutions like the University of California at San Diego help fuel bio-tech growth.

Because of a large military presence, national defense is another significant local industry. San Diego is also a headquarters for the wireless cellular technology industry, and one major player, Qualcomm Incorporated, is the largest private sector technology employer (not counting hospitals) in the United States. San Diego's economy also relies heavily on its port, which has the only submarine and shipbuilding yard on the West Coast, not to mention the naval base.

"Sin" Fernando Valley

In the 1970s, the San Fernando Valley began its journey to becoming the leading producer of adult entertainment films in the country. Mischievously dubbed "Silicone Valley" or "San Pornando Valley," it's estimated that more than 85 percent of the adult movie and video production in North America takes place in the San Fernando Valley. It's a multi-billion–dollar industry, and unlike other film production, doesn't look to be running off to Canada anytime soon. Although Canada gives tax rebates and other incentives to foreign film companies, its tax regulations specifically bar subsidies for skin flicks.

Gold—Southern California–Style

If you're interested in the history of the once-thriving, now swiftly dwindling citrus industry of California, you could do worse than to stop by California Citrus Historic State Park, located in Riverside. It's a fitting place because it's where a few imported branches of a naval orange tree launched the industry. The 400-acre park is modeled after a city park circa 1900 and strives to give a feeling of the time when citrus created its own mini gold rush. The park is full of demonstration groves of every conceivable kind of citrus, but it's also got plenty of other plants evocative of the era, such as palm trees, eucalyptus and wisteria. As one visitor pointed out, they, along with citrus, are very much part of the romance of Southern California. Funny thing, though—not one of them happens to be native.

The Ground Beneath Their Feet

It's worth keeping in mind that Los Angeles' destiny was founded on oil and that the L.A. Basin is still the richest oil field in North America and the second richest in the world. Although the last significant onshore drilling in the L.A. Basin was done in the 1960s and '70s, there was still a lot of oil in the ground, and smaller niche companies came in to extract a little more. There are oil wells everywhere, including 20 or so derricks pumping right by the

famed Farmer's Market and one at the entrance to the enormous parking lot of the Beverly Center shopping mall. Some of them are a little harder to see, of course. These days, people are not as, well, thrilled to see working oil derricks as they once were, and drillers often go to some lengths to disguise them. The derrick at Pico Boulevard and Genesee Avenue is disguised to look like an office building.

DID YOU KNOW?

"Tech Coast" is the nickname that think tank president Tim Cooley has tried to brand Southern California with to give it a name recognition similar to Silicon Valley and to make people realize that the area between northern San Diego County and Santa Barbara has one of the highest concentrations of research and development groups in the world. But so far, although regional papers have picked up on the name, people elsewhere tend not to have latched on to it. Never mind. Southern California has stopped being an area dominated by aerospace and defense and has become a much more diversified player in the global economy.

"Internestic"

That's the term a former consul general of California in Los Angeles used to describe Canada-U.S. relations because they are unique, being neither completely international nor completely domestic. In 2004, there were 110,000 jobs in California that were in some way involved in doing business with Canada.

By his reckoning, the U.S. and Canada trade about one million dollars worth of goods every *second*. And though 39 U.S. states list Canada as their primary export market, California leads the pack with $23 billion in goods traded between California and Canada in 2002, up from $11.8 billion a mere four years before in 1998. Telecommunications, computers and agriculture all factor hugely in California's exports to Canada.

In 2002, 900,000 Canadian tourists spent over $540 million in California, but California came close to repaying the compliment by sending one million tourists over the northern border who spent close to $500 million.

Canada provides one-third of all the softwood lumber used in U.S. construction, a particularly important fact in a state that, according to the California Building Industry Association, had a record 210,527 housing starts in 2004, a 15-year high. With each house using on average $40,000 worth of wood, that's a lot of Canadian log felling.

DID YOU KNOW?

There's one industry in which California-Canada relations haven't always been so felicitous: the film industry. Hollywood has been up in arms in recent years over the phenomenon of what it terms "runaway productions," meaning film productions that have taken off to Canada and other countries that help shave off the costs of production with attractive subsidies. The solution proposed by legislators from California? Let's offer our own subsidies. Yeah, that's the ticket.

SOUTHERN CALIFORNIA: ONE GREAT BIG FREEWAY

The One that Started It All

The first freeway in California opened on January 1, 1940. State Route 110, otherwise known as the Pasadena Freeway or the Arroyo Seco Freeway, extends from Los Angeles to Pasadena. It was built in an era when there was less traffic and cars were slower, so it is one of the more dangerous freeways because its lanes are narrower, there are no shoulders and its ramps are shorter, making it harder to accelerate to the speed of traffic flow.

Why Are They Screaming?

The Ventura Freeway, a.k.a. Route 101, is the principal east-west route through Ventura County and the southern portion of the San Fernando Valley. It begins in Ventura and continues on to Pasadena, although it is signed as California State Route 134 after intersecting with the Hollywood Freeway. In the portion that runs through Ventura County, it is officially named the Screaming Eagles Highway in honor of the 101 Airborne Division of the United States Army.

A Bit of Congestion

The Santa Monica Freeway, or Route 10, cuts through the heart of downtown L.A. Although construction of the Century Freeway helped by providing an alternative route to LAX, the Santa Monica Freeway is still one of the busiest freeways in the world. All three of its main interchanges are routinely listed among the top 10 most congested interchanges in the world!

Unsafe at Any Speed

Coming all the way from Northern California, Route 5, some-times lauded as the Golden State Freeway, begins where I-5 and California State Highway 99 converge at the southernmost point of the San Joaquin Valley. Soon it climbs steeply to the Tejon Pass through the Tehachapi Mountains. The Grapevine, named for the little town there, was notorious for accidents until it was smoothed and graded for Interstate 5.

DID YOU KNOW?

The Grapevine may have been graded, but that doesn't neces-sarily make it safe. This pass over the Tehachapis is not really human made—it's a creation of the nearby San Andreas Fault, as are the Cajon Pass and the San Gorgonio Pass. Any major slip-page on the fault nearby could easily play havoc with any of these roads. Forget about Universal Studios. This would be the ulti-mate scary ride—and not one I have any interest on being on.

The Slow Lane? Take Your Pick

The San Diego Freeway, or Route 405, slices through the San Fernando Valley and the Westside and then curves east towards Orange County. Because it is one of the principal north-south freeways in California and connects so many cities in Los Angeles County and Orange County, taking up the burden where Route 5 leaves off, it is one of the busiest and most con-gested freeways in the world. One quip is that it's called the 405 because traffic on it goes only four or five miles an hour. At some points in peak hours, this is no exaggeration.

DID YOU KNOW?

The San Diego Freeway was the scene of one of the most famous, or rather infamous, low-speed chases in history. It was this freeway that O.J. Simpson and his friend and teammate Al Cowling took to after Simpson was accused of the murder of his wife, Nicole Brown Simpson, and waiter Ronald Goldman. Simpson was pursued for hours by police in one of the most televised car chases ever. Eventually, he took the Sunset Boulevard exit and returned to his estate in Brentwood, where he surrendered to police.

That Ever-Increasing Commute

The Hollywood Freeway (Route 101 and State Route 170) is one of the busiest freeways in the U.S. Its main route is over the Cahuenga Pass, and it connects the Los Angeles Basin with the San Fernando Valley.

Stack 'em Up!

The interchange where the Hollywood Freeway meets with the Harbor, Pasadena and Santa Ana freeways is now officially known as the Bill Keene Memorial Interchange in honor of a veteran traffic reporter (how appropriate), but it is also referred to as the Four Level Interchange or simply the Stack. It was the first stack interchange in the world. This type of interchange has one major road crossing another by means of a bridge, with connector roads crossing on two farther levels. It's the best style of interchange for the driver and in terms of carrying capacity, but it is also one of the most expensive to build in terms of land and construction.

Getting the Goods Inland

The Harbor Freeway, a portion of Interstate 110, is one of the principal north-south routes in Los Angeles County. It runs from the port at San Pedro to the Santa Monica Freeway south of Los Angeles. The Harbor Freeway is one of the main ways for freight to get from the port of Los Angeles to warehouses and rail yards farther inland.

Premium Destinations

Another major freeway that takes off from the Bill Keene Memorial Interchange, the Santa Ana Freeway (Interstate 5, which becomes U.S. Route 101), connects Los Angeles with its southeastern suburbs. Because it passes both Disneyland and Angels Stadium in Anaheim, that portion of the route is one of the most seriously congested freeways in Southern California. In fact, the interchange where the Santa Ana, Garden Grove and Orange freeways connect was nicknamed the "Orange Crush Interchange," and *Guinness World Records 2002* cited it as the most complex road interchange in the world, claiming it to be the intersection of 34 different routes. But construction in the late 1990s and early 2000s has greatly improved its efficiency.

Seaside Drive

No list of Southern California highways would be complete without mention of the Pacific Coast Highway, or PCH, which is surely one of the most beautiful stretches of highway in the world. It is officially designated as that stretch of State Route 1 between Dana Point in the south and Oxnard in the north, but it parallels the California coast through the famous beachfronts of Santa Monica, Malibu and beyond.

AIRPORTS

Not Lax by a Long Shot

☞ Los Angeles International Airport, often referred to by its IATA airport code designation, LAX (pronounced as if spelled out, not "lax"), is the primary airport serving Los Angeles.

☞ It is the fifth busiest in the world by passenger traffic and sixth busiest by cargo traffic.

☞ In 2004, it served 60 million passengers and moved over two million tons of freight.

☞ LAX began its existence in 1928 as Mines Field when the City of Los Angeles purchased 640 rural acres in Westchester for an airfield.

☛ The first hangar was built in 1929, and it was dedicated as the official airport of Los Angeles in 1930.

☛ Commercial airline service started in 1946.

☛ It didn't become Los Angeles International Airport until 1949.

☛ The first jet service began in 1959, transporting passengers between Los Angeles and New York.

☛ LAX has expanded steadily since its humble beginnings; it currently has eight terminals and occupies 3425 acres, extending right to edge of the Pacific Ocean.

The Little Engine That Could
Van Nuys Airport is the busiest general aviation—meaning non-military and with no scheduled flights—airport in the world. With just two runways side by side, it had 448,681 aircraft movements in 2004 and handled 1400 operations daily in 2006. By comparison, LAX handles 1700 operations daily.

Duke's Place

John Wayne Airport is located in Orange County and was in fact called Orange County Airport until 1979, when it was given its current name to honor the famous film star, who had lived in Newport and had died that year. It started its life in 1923 as an airstrip for a flying school run by Eddie Martin. John Wayne Airport has one of the shortest runways of any major U.S. airport, which means size does matter here. Nothing larger than a Boeing 757 is permitted. Even for smaller aircraft, the short runway makes takeoff quite challenging. John Wayne Airport is only 14 miles from Disneyland, while LAX is 35 miles away. In an area whose roads are plagued by chronic traffic congestion, this location is quite a plus for the smaller airport.

In 2004, Chris Norby of the county board of supervisors suggested changing the name of the airport to The O.C. Airport, John Wayne Field, but was thwarted in his plans to give a nod to the popular television series by the complaints of the outraged citizenry. Good thing. *The O.C.* was cancelled in early 2007. Meanwhile, John Wayne's legend lives on.

 John Wayne Airport has another claim to fame: it was the home of the first commercial drag strip. The Santa Ana Drag was held on one of the runways every Sunday from June 19, 1950, until it was closed in 1959. The reason for the closure? Just too many flights coming in.

An Airport by Any Other Name... Would Still Be the Same Airport

For a small airport, this one has certainly had a lot of names. It began as United Airport in 1930 and was the largest commercial airport for many years, until the Los Angeles Municipal Airport began commercial flights in 1946.

Its name was changed to Union Air Terminal in 1934, but it was bought by Lockheed in 1940, which quickly changed its name to—guess what?—Lockheed Air Terminal. Lockheed changed the character of the small airport too, as the company's aircraft manufacture at the airport developed many military aircraft. However, by 1967, Lockheed was looking for a little more pizzazz and renamed it Hollywood-Burbank Airport.

Lockheed then sold the airport to the Burbank-Glendale-Pasadena Airport Authority in 1978, which is how it got the truly cumbersome moniker of Burbank-Glendale-Pasadena Airport.

When Bob Hope, who had lived in nearby Toluca Lake, died in 2003, naturally the airport authority jumped at the chance to honor him. The airport was renamed Bob Hope Airport on December 17, 2003, the 100th anniversary of the Wright Brothers' first flight and also the 100th anniversary of the year Hope was born. Maybe this name will stick.

DID YOU KNOW?

It was from Bob Hope Airport on September 21, 2005, that Jet Blue Airways Flight 292 took off only to discover that one of its front wheels had failed to retract and was jammed at a 90° angle to its proper direction. Because news helicopters captured this problem at takeoff and aired the footage on cable news, the country, if not the world, watched the plane circle for hours in dread and fascination until, thanks to the skill—and luck—of the pilot, the plane landed safely at Los Angeles International Airport.

DID YOU KNOW?

In 1988, the heavy metal band Megadeth was given permission to film their music video for "In My Darkest Hour" at this airport. The filming had been heavily advertised, and metal fans turned out in droves to watch. Perhaps not altogether surprisingly, the film shoot turned rowdy, with fans spray-painting planes and leaving broken bottles on the runway. Airport authorities may well have thought it was *their* darkest hour.

Lucky Lindy's Landing Field

San Diego International Airport is the second-busiest single runway airport in the world, with only Gatwick Airport in London taking precedence. It is also called Lindbergh Field because the plane in which Lindbergh flew the world's first transatlantic flight, *The Spirit of St. Louis*, was built in San Diego by Ryan Airlines.

RIDING THE RAILS

Last of the Great Railway Stations

Or so Los Angeles Union Station is often referred to as, anyway. Built in 1939, it was just in time to be the perfect arrival and departure point for World War II soldiers, as well as for glamorous movie stars. It is considered one of the finest examples of Mission Style architecture. Once the terminus of three great railway lines, the Union Pacific Railroad, the Southern Pacific Railroad and the Atchison, Topeka and Santa Fe Railway, it fell dormant when train travel declined but has had a small renaissance since the Metrolink made it a hub of Southern California's commuter traffic, and Amtrak's lines began to do a more flourishing business. It has an almost cathedral-like interior, with beamed ceilings 52 feet off the ground, marble floors and Aztec-influenced inlaid tile.

The restaurant at Los Angeles Union Station, considered an architectural gem for its sleek, Moderne style, was designed by Mary Colter, an influential architect of the Southwest. She did much of her work for Fred Harvey, an entrepreneur who built restaurants, hotels and souvenir shops for several major railroads, including the Atchison, Topeka and Santa Fe Railway. This restaurant was the last Harvey house attached to a railroad station.

DID YOU KNOW?

San Diego Union Station is another great example of Mission Style public architecture. With twin campaniles, it looks much more like a Spanish mission than do most train stations I can think of.

The Shortest Railroad in the World?

Angels Flight is the name of two funicular railroads that have climbed downtown Los Angeles' Bunker Hill. Although they used the same two historic cars, Sinai and Olivet, the two railroads existed on slightly different sites and used different track and haulage systems.

The first Angels Flight, which opened in 1901, would not have met current funicular standards, but it operated for 68 years with a good safety record and was only closed in 1969 because of the redevelopment of Bunker Hill.

The second Angels Flight opened on a new site in 1996 but had to close again on February 1, 2001, when Sinai, near the top of the hill, reversed direction and went out of control back down the hill, crashing into Olivet and killing one passenger and injuring seven others. It was later determined that maintenance on Sinai's emergency break had been negligent and that the two cars had neither a safety cable nor a track break, either of which would have prevented the accident. The site is scheduled to be reopened in summer of 2007. You go first.

Popular crime writer Michael Connelly, who often features authentic Los Angeles locales in his novels, actually named one of his books after Angels Flight. One of the cars was the scene of the opening crime.

The Red Cars and the Yellow Cars

The Los Angeles Railway was a narrow gauge railroad that operated in the L.A. area between 1901 and 1963. Unofficially, these were known as the "yellow cars," partly to distinguish them from the "red cars" of the Pacific Electric Railway, which connected L.A. with more outlying cities such as Santa Ana and San Bernardino. Although, in the age of the automobile, the streetcar system was in decline, the decision of a holding company headed by General Motors to dismantle the yellow car lines and replace them with buses has long rankled the public, which continues to view this move as a conspiracy to sell more cars and buses.

A DASH OF PORT(S)

The Shallow End

The Port of Los Angeles at San Pedro Bay, together with the neighboring Port of Long Beach, comprises one of the world's largest human-made ports, with 35 miles of intricate waterfront. It handles billions and billions of dollars worth of cargo every year. No one would guess that in its beginnings it was only a shallow mudflat, too soft to even support a wharf. Visiting ships had to ferry all their goods ashore or beach themselves. But Phineas Banning, who owned a stagecoach line to Salt Lake City, was one of those entrepreneurial visionaries who seem to be so prevalent in the Southland. He decided to dredge the channel to a depth of 10 feet, and the port managed to handle 50,000 tons of shipping that year.

The Deep End

Port Hueneme in Ventura County near Oxnard is the only deep-water port between the port of Long Beach and the Port of San Francisco, and it is the only military port between San Diego and Puget Sound. It is the west coast home of the Construction Battalion, better known as the Seabees, of naval fame.

STATISTICALLY SPEAKING

Doctor, How Long Have We Got?

☛ The life expectancy at birth for the total population of California in 2004 was 80.2 years, an increase of 0.6 years from 2003.

☛ The life expectancy at birth of Californians was 2.3 years longer than that of the U.S. population as a whole.

☛ In 2004, California females had a life expectancy 4.7 years longer than males, a considerably narrower difference than the 6.7-year gap found as recently as 1990.

☛ Ninety-five percent of Californians live to age 50, and 90 percent survive to age 60.

☛ Latino male mortality is lower than white male mortality, except between the ages of five and nine due to accidents, and between 15 and 19 due, sadly, to homicide.

☛ East Indians have the longest life expectancy in the state at 84.3 years, while Laotian Asians have a life expectancy of only 75.3 years.

☛ Infant mortality rates among African-Americans are higher than for any other ethnicity—almost 13 deaths per 1000 births, compared to roughly five deaths for both Latinos and whites and only four deaths for Asians. But infant mortality varies widely by subgroup in the Asian community. For those of Japanese ancestry it's only two per 1000, while Laotians have 11 per 1000.

☛ A surprising and somewhat baffling fact that came out of the 2000 census is that foreign-born residents of California live longer than their native-born counterparts in almost every ethnic subgroup. The difference in life expectancy between foreign-born blacks and those born in California is five years, while it is three years for Latinos and two years for whites.

☛ Out of 19 groups, only California-born Asians had an advantage over their immigrant counterparts, overall by about two years.

☛ The most drastic comparison of extremes is that a U.S.-born Asian female outlives a U.S.-born black male by an average of *20* years.

DID YOU KNOW?

Because ultimately there is probably Oscars trivia about everything, we can offer up this little tidbit here. According to Michael Marmot, who wrote about his groundbreaking work on social hierarchies in *The Status Syndrome,* there's more at stake to winning the Oscar than we ever knew. It turns out that Oscar winners live longer than the nominees—by an average of about four years. On average, those who take the Oscar home live to be 79.7 years old, while those who lack those little gold statues live, on average, to be only 75.8.

MEDICAL MIRACLES

The Resolute Researchers of UCLA

☛ In 1956, the first open heart surgery in the western United States was performed.

☛ In 1964, a test was developed that has since become the international standard for tissue typing. No organ transplant can be performed unless this test has been given.

☛ In 1974, positron emission tomography (PET) was developed. This imaging technology visualizes metabolic changes in the brain and body. Michael Phelps invented the PET scan. He was awarded the Enrico Fermi Prize, the government's oldest science and technology prize, in 1999.

☛ The first total shoulder replacement was performed in 1976.

☛ In 1981, a new technique was developed called retroperfusion, which uses a pump to oxygenate blood to restore damaged heart tissue directly after a heart attack.

☛ In 1985, the first non-surgical kidney stone removal on the west coast was performed using a lithotripter, a device that pulverizes kidney and gall stones by passing shock waves through patients as they sit in a tub of water.

☛ The first live-donor liver transplant was successfully performed in 1993.

☛ In 2000, Dr. Larry Zipursky discovered that a single gene that controls the neuron guidance receptor in the fruit fly can generate 38,016 different but related proteins. This was an extreme case of what is known as "alternative splicing," and since it now turns out to be more the rule than the exception, it confounded a 50-year-old model of genetics that said "one gene, one protein." Now it looks more like "one gene, many proteins."

☛ In 2001, a UCLA plastic surgeon named Mark Hedrick revealed that his research team had successfully harvested stem cells from fat removed by liposuction, and had grown bone, muscle, cartilage and fat tissue.

☛ In 2002, Dr. Andrew Leuchter used quantitative electro-encephalogram (EEG) images to show changes in brain function in depressed patients who had been given a placebo.

☛ A vaccine that stops the progression of Type 1 diabetes was demonstrated in 2003, the culmination of 20 years of research.

☛ In 2004, UCLA research showed for the first time that air pollutants alone may cause asthma attacks.

Intercontinental Imaging

UCLA and the University of Queensland in Australia have teamed up to create the first three-dimensional images of the progress of Alzheimer's. MRI scans were given to a dozen Alzheimers patients over the course of 18 months. The images were fed into a computer, which merged them into a basic model. Then the computer morphed one image into the next, creating a very scary kind of animation showing the rapid invasion and progress of the disease across the brain. Although a single MRI scan can show dead brain functions, this new model can show the rate of progression and how well a patient is responding to a particular medication. Doctors will no longer have to rely on symptoms to make medical decisions.

Saving Tiny Lives

In 2006, UC San Diego Medical Center performed the first in-utero surgery in Southern California. A procedure known as fetoscopy was used to correct a condition known as twin-to-twin transfusion syndrome, in which one twin gets too much blood and the other not enough. Without the surgery, which closes blood vessels on the surface of the placenta so that the twins no longer share blood vessels, neither twin would have survived.

I Can See!

USC researcher Mark Humayun led a research team in 2002 that put artificial retina implants into the eyes of six patients. Sixteen electrodes attached to the retina work in tandem with an external camera and video processing system to restore partial sight to people who suffer macular degeneration, in which light receptors lose the ability to process light. A second generation of implants, which contain 60 electrodes and will result in higher image resolution, was approved in February 2007.

It's Not Rocket Science—but It Is Helpful

In what must be a unique collaboration, former rocket scientists from NASA's Jet Propulsion Laboratory in Pasadena have teamed up with doctors and medical centers to help research and brainstorm new medical advances. These retirees have formed a group called Volunteer Professionals for Medical Advancement and have made advances in the following areas:

☛ an automated oxygen enrichment program for premature babies. Manually controlled oxygen systems have sometimes been known to harm infants' eyes and impair brain and lung development.

☛ solving a problem with a stent that had been known to cause heart attacks. They introduced an electropolishing process that had been used in the space industry but was relatively unknown to doctors, which produces a super smooth surface. Blood clotting was practically eliminated with the improved stent.

☛ creating an advanced database private network for pediatricians to compare information nationwide. Working with the Children's Hospital of Los Angeles, the scientists estimated that extended use of the database could lower health care costs by as much as 20 to 30 percent.

BELOW THE CURVE

Not-So-Fun Facts About California Literacy

☛ According to the National Adult Literacy Survey, two million native speakers in California are functionally illiterate, which means that they are unable to read and write in English or compute and solve problems at a level necessary to secure a job and function in the workplace.

☛ According to the CaliforniaDepartment of Education, 33 percent of California's children will not finish high school. (Yes, that's *one-third*, folks.)

☛ Twenty-four percent of adults are at the lowest literacy level.

☛ Because of the scope of the problem, there are many groups dedicated to the problem of illiteracy. California Literacy Inc. was founded in 1956, making it the nation's oldest statewide volunteer literacy organization. The Literacy Network of Greater Los Angeles has as its motto, "Promoting literacy throughout the Southland." And the San Diego Council on Literacy is working towards a more literate community in San Diego County.

Lagging Behind

California currently ranks above only Louisiana and Mississippi on student achievement as it is rated by national standardized tests. Although we might leap to the assumption that this is because of the high percentage of minority families, many of whom come from low-income circumstances and sometimes must learn English as a second language, in fact, controlling for students' background, California scores *lowest* of any state. Still, California students have made gains on these tests when it comes to math and reading. The improvement among fourth graders in the last seven years has been greater than that of fourth graders in other states.

Teaching Deficit

California has the second highest student to teacher ratio in the nation, even after a big campaign in 1996 to reduce ratios for K–3 and for the ninth grade. California K–12 has an average of 20.9 students per teacher, as opposed to the national average of 16.1.

DID YOU KNOW?

Only 46 percent of California school districts require teachers to have full standard certification, in contrast to 82 percent nationally.

Salary Deficit

When adjusted for inflation, the real average annual salary for a teacher in 2000–01 was about the same as it was in 1969–70. In today's dollars, the adjusted annual average salary comes to about $39,000, placing California last among the five largest states and 32nd in the nation.

Fallen Funding

The decline of California's K–12 system is paralleled by the decline of per-pupil financial support over the last three decades. It began about 30 years ago when the state began to implement school finance reform that shifted the responsibility for school funding from local sources to the state. Although this reform narrowed the gap between rich and poor students and made spending per student more equal across the state, it tended to lower spending per student overall. In the 1969–70 school year, the state was spending $400 annually per student above the national average. In 1999–2000, it was spending $600 below that average. In 2001, California ranked 27th in per-pupil spending.

Fertility Factor

As far as other factors affecting student education go, the pregnancy rate for 15- to 17-year-olds is higher than in any other state except the District of Columbia, though on an optimistic note, this rate is also falling faster than in any other state.

At Least They've Got Their Health

To end on a further optimistic note, the California youth has a comparatively low use of cigarettes and alcohol when compared to the national average.

SCHOOL IS COOL!

Oldest Schools

☛ Although Northern California takes the honors for oldest university in the state, higher education came to the Southland when the University of Southern California opened its doors in 1880 with 53 students and 10 teachers.

☛ In 1885, Southern California opened its first medical school, also at USC.

☛ The Southern Branch of the University of California, later to become UCLA, opened in 1919.

☛ Loyola High School is a Jesuit Preparatory School. It's the oldest high school in Southern California, having been founded in 1865 as St. Vincent's College. It is the region's oldest educational institution, predating the University of California system.

☛ Manual Arts High School was founded in 1910. It's one of the oldest schools in Los Angeles, and the oldest one still standing on its original site.

Higher Learning

Clark Kerr developed the Master Plan for Higher Education in 1960. It defined the role of the three types of state higher education then in existence. The top one-eighth of graduating high school seniors would be guaranteed a place at one of the University of California campuses. The top third would be able to enter the California State system. The community colleges would accept all applications. In addition, it said that graduates of the two-year community colleges would be eligible to transfer to either a UC or state college by virtue of their community college work.

The plan, giving each portion of the higher education system a mission, was a catalyst for a great surge of development in California's higher education system. Many people credit the higher education system as a foundation for California's place in the world economy. In particular, the highly skilled technological learning required for the computer industry, pharmaceuticals and bio-technology has been supported by the investment in higher education as thought through by the Clark Kerr plan.

So Many Choices!

Five of the University of California campuses are located in Southern California:

- ☛ UC Los Angeles (UCLA)
- ☛ UC San Diego
- ☛ UC Irvine
- ☛ UC Santa Barbara
- ☛ UC Riverside

Southern California has 10 state college campuses:

- ☛ Channel Islands
- ☛ Fullerton
- ☛ Los Angeles
- ☛ Pomona
- ☛ San Diego
- ☛ Dominguez Hills
- ☛ Long Beach
- ☛ Northridge
- ☛ San Bernardino
- ☛ San Marco

And a hefty portion of the state's 109 community colleges are in Southern California, all of which offer a two-year associate of arts degree. In addition, there are many prestigious private colleges, notably the University of Southern California, the colleges of the Claremont Consortium, the University of San Diego, Loyola Marymount and Chapman College, to name but a few.

Trojans vs. Bruins

The UCLA-USC rivalry is one of the most intense in the country, at least partly because the two schools are so close to each other—only 10 miles apart. Inevitably, the rivalry centers around football but ends up affecting all other sports teams as well, especially because the Lexus Gauntlet, a 150-pound trophy modeled after a real medieval gauntlet, is given by Lexus, the car manufacturer, each year to whichever school wins the most of the 18 competitive sports for which they each field teams. But even other groups get into the rivalry. The ROTC, or Reserve Officers Training Corps, of each school takes part in a flag football game called the Blood Bowl—no explanation needed there—and the two school papers also have a flag game, which is—a little more mysteriously—also called the Blood Bowl. There was also a game called the Band Bowl between the two rival marching bands, but after fights and theft, it was decided that this particular game should be suspended. Who knew that band members were such hooligans?

Taking It Too Far

The Victory Bell is a 295-pound bell that is originally from a Southern Pacific freight locomotive. It was given to the UCLA student body by their alumni association in 1939. During football games, the UCLA cheerleaders would clang the bell after every point. But while UCLA was playing Washington in 1941, six members of the Sig Ep fraternity of USC infiltrated UCLA's cheering section, loaded the bell onto a truck and then drove off with it. The bell was hidden for over a year in the Hollywood Hills, Santa Ana and even a haystack.

Eventually the rivalry got out of hand, with UCLA painting the statue of Tommy Trojan, the USC mascot, blue and USC burning its initials into the UCLA lawn. Finally, the USC president threatened to cancel the USC-UCLA game if the bell was not returned. A compromise was finally reached in November 1942: the bell would become a trophy, going to whichever team had won that year.

Film School

USC's School of Cinema-Television is the oldest film school in the world. It was founded in 1928 as a joint venture of USC and the Academy of Motion Picture Arts and Sciences. Its starting faculty included *Birth of a Nation* director D.W. Griffith and actor Douglas Fairbanks. With such roots, it's no wonder that it's the most "Hollywood" of the three biggest L.A. film schools.

Walt and Roy Disney founded CalArts in 1961. Perhaps because of the Disney connection, it is a leader in animated film and has connections with the New York Museum of Modern Art, where it's held some recent major exhibitions. During the dark days after the golden era in animation and before the form revived again in the 1990s, the school had access to many master animators from both Disney Studios and Warner Brothers, who would otherwise, let's face it, have been left languishing.

The UCLA School of Theatre Arts and Television is one of the only public film schools in the country, and hence, at least for California residents, a bargain. It doesn't have the lavish facilities of the other two schools, but it does all right with Hollywood castoffs, such as Disney's old animation tables and a set from the TV show *Friends.* Its film archive is the second largest in the country.

CLASSIC CALIFORNIA

When Alexander Payne won the L.A. Film Festival Award, he said, "I learned everything I know about new movies by watching old movies at UCLA."

NOTABLE TEACHERS

Taking the Risk

Erin Gruwell, twice named California Teacher of the Year, as well as the recipient of numerous other awards, began her career in Long Beach in a class of "high-risk" kids. Appalled to discover that they had never heard of the Holocaust, and then further shocked to discover how many had been (quite literally) scarred by shootings, she began a program to teach tolerance, which included the students writing about their own lives. The story she told in *The Freedom Writers Diary* has since gone on to become a big Hollywood movie.

Higher Math

Jaime Escalante was another noted educator made famous by a movie, this one *Stand and Deliver*. After emigrating from Bolivia, he taught high school math at Garfield High in Los Angeles and, like Gruwell, was initially demoralized by the low level of learning skills he found there. But eventually he started teaching a calculus class, and the students did so well that in 1982, 18 of them passed the Advanced Placement exam in calculus. This was so unheard of at the time from this particular East L.A. school district that the Educational Testing Service suspected the students of cheating and asked 14 of them to retake the test; 12 did, and did well enough to have their scores reinstated.

DIVIDING THE PIE

Red or Blue?

Although only the two major parties, the Democratic Party and the Republican Party, have representation in the State Legislature and the United States Congress, the Green Party did get a representative into the State Assembly during the 1990s. In addition to these three, there are four other parties that officially qualify for ballot status.

Going Green

The Green Party, though fielding a few heavy hitters, has had most of its success at the local level of politics, particularly on non-partisan ballots where candidates are not identified as affiliated with a particular party. The California chapter's commitments include ecological sustainability, grassroots democracy and nonviolence.

Liberty

The only other California party positioned to be a real third party contender is the Libertarian Party. It has more than

200,000 members at the national level, currently has scores of members in office at the local and county level in California and has been around since 1971, proving it has staying power.

Independence

The American Independent Party was started on July 8, 1967, in California by Bill Shearer to form a new conservative party under which Governor George C. Wallace could run, and California had the population necessary to get the 66,000-plus voter registrations to do it. Political theorists suggest that the party remains on the ballot because many voters register as members, thinking that by doing so they are registering as "independent." In fact, the group has a pretty strong agenda, including reducing immigration, terminating international trade agreements like NAFTA and getting rid of the federal income tax.

Peace and Freedom

The Peace and Freedom Party was created in 1967 in opposition to the Vietnam War, and its initial registration drive began at a demonstration against President Lyndon Johnson at the Century City Plaza in Los Angeles. It eventually attained ballot status in 13 other states, but it was unable to sustain the required votes to remain on ballots. Even in California, it has wavered on and off the ballot in recent years. But in the November 2006 election, two candidates, Elizabeth Barron for Controller and Tom Condit for Insurance Commissioner, each received more than two percent of the vote, ensuring the party's position on the ballot for the next four years.

Justice

The United States Natural Law Party, though a national political party, was funded almost exclusively by Maharishi Mahesh Yogi, the leader of the Transcendental Meditation movement. It disbanded nationally in May 2004, though it remains active in a few states.

VOTING TRENDS

Republican vs. Democrat

From the 1950s until 1992, California voted for the Republican presidential candidate in every election except that of 1964. But the combination of more Latino voters, who as a group still tend to vote for Democrats, plus the flight of the Republican middle class to more inland states such as Montana and Utah in the 1980s and '90s, has shifted the balance of power towards the Democratic Party.

Ace Ventura

Ventura County in Southern California is one of the two California counties that come closest to perfect scores when it comes to voting for the winner in presidential elections, the other being Merced County up north. Both counties have voted for the winning presidential candidate in 22 out of the past 24 elections, including the 2004 election that let George W. Bush stay in office. Voters have registered in nearly equal numbers as Democrats and Republicans, making them very similar to Ohio and Pennsylvania, states that act as national bellwethers in presidential elections.

Rise of the Latino Voter

The Latino share of California voting has nearly doubled in the last 15 years. In 1990, it represented 10 percent of the vote in the state, rising to 19 percent in 2005. Latinos have accounted for 70 percent of the net growth in the registered California voter population since 1990. It is a trend that's likely to continue. Latinos still favor top-of-the-ticket Democratic candidates over Republican ones by more than a two-to-one margin.

The Coastal/Inland Divide

Recent elections reveal that the gap is widening between coastal California and inland California. Coastal voters make up 71 percent of California's voting population. They favor Democratic candidates by double-digit margins. A large proportion of coastal voters tends to be either registered Democrats or non-partisans, and a large share of the demographic is liberal, college educated, high income and never married.

In contrast, while inland voters also favor their candidates by double-digit margins, their candidates tend to be Republican. The inland population tends to be represented by conservative, Protestant (especially of the born-again variety), married, non-college educated and lower income voters.

Voting by Mail

Voting by mail extends the window of opportunity for making your vote count from a mere 13 hours on Election Day to a three- to four-week period. It allows voters to sidestep Election Day hassles, such as bad weather, long lines and trying to figure out where their voting booth is. Voting by mail allows voters to have all the aids they need right at hand while they try to sort through the growing number of propositions they must tackle every year. The sheer convenience and ease of voting by mail ensures that it will be an increasing trend in the future, although there are still many people who enjoy going down to the precinct and voting in the more traditional way. In fact, increased mail ballot voting seems to have halted the long-term decline in California voting, as evidenced by the higher than expected turnouts in the 2003, 2004 and 2005 elections.

NOTABLE FIGURES

The Governator

I doubt that there were many before the summer of 2003 that could have imagined, let alone predicted, that a former body-builder from Graz, Austria, turned multi-millionaire and mega celebrity, who had never before held public office, would end up as governor of California. But that's exactly what happened when Republican opponents found sufficient funds to gather the 900,000 petition signatures required to hold a recall election on Governor Gray Davis. This drama captured the (often horrified) attention of the nation, and the term the "Governator," combining Arnold Schwarzenegger's hit movie role as the Terminator and his will to govern into one title, became a nickname for him.

The Teflon President

That celebrity should translate into votes along with some careful campaign management should have come as no surprise. After all, California is the state that launched the political career of another Hollywood movie star. Like his successor in office, Ronald Reagan was actually born elsewhere, but his long career as an actor and then as president of the Screen Actor's Guild give him a prominent place in Southern California history. He became a successful California governor and ended up in the White House.

DID YOU KNOW?

It was Representative Patricia Schroeder from Colorado who was largely responsible for Reagan's nickname. She said, "He's just like a Teflon frying pan. Nothing sticks to him."

And the Beat Goes On

In yet another example of a celebrity catching the political bug, singer, songwriter and producer Sonny Bono, famous for his part in the singing duo Sonny and Cher, first threw his hat into the political ring when he was frustrated with the red tape involved in opening a Palm Springs restaurant. In 1988, he was elected mayor of Palm Springs by a landslide. He was then elected to the House of Representatives in 1994, where he notably championed the cause of saving the Salton Sea, California's largest lake.

Tricky Dick

Richard Milhouse Nixon was born in Yorba Linda, making him the only native-born Californian ever to be elected to the presidency. He ran for governor of California in 1962 after being narrowly defeated in the 1960 presidential election by John F. Kennedy, but he lost that, too. He ran his first successful campaign for the presidency in 1968 from a New York power base. During his term in office, he withdrew troops from Vietnam and is credited with re-establishing diplomatic relations with China, as well as following a policy of détente with the Soviet Union. But though he had a resounding election victory in 1972, by 1974, the Watergate scandal broke, and, faced with impeachment, Nixon became the first, and so far only, president to resign from office.

DID YOU  KNOW?

The nickname "Tricky Dick" was given to Nixon by Helen Gahagan Douglas, a former actress and member of the House of Representatives who was running against him for the Senate seat. Nixon, trying to smear her with Communist associations, accused her of being "pink right down to her underwear." She responded by labeling him Tricky Dick. Nixon was far from being a Teflon congressman. He won the election, but the name stuck.

One of the Supremes

Earl Warren was a true son of California. He was born in Los Angeles, grew up in Bakersfield and went to college and law school in Berkeley. In 1942, he was elected governor of California under the Republican banner, but in 1946, he accomplished the unusual feat of winning the Democratic, Republican and Progressive Party primaries and thus ran for his second term unopposed. President Dwight D. Eisenhower appointed Warren chief justice of the Supreme Court, where Warren confounded everyone by turning out to be surprisingly liberal. Eisenhower, who had wanted someone more conservative, said of the appointment, "Biggest damned-fool mistake I ever made."

The Man from Chhajulwadi

In 1956, Dilip Singh Saund was elected to the U.S. Congress from the 29th District of California, which then consisted of Riverside County and Imperial County. A Sikh born in Chhajulwadi, Punjab Province, India, in 1899, he was the first Asian (or Asian-American—he became a naturalized citizen in 1949) to be elected to Congress.

A TALE FROM
THE CALIFORNIA
UNDERGROUND

S.L.A. Kidnapping

On February 4, 1974, Patricia Campbell Hearst, an heiress of the Hearst newspaper dynasty, was kidnapped out of her apartment by a group that soon revealed itself to be the Symbionese Liberation Army. Led by Donald DeFreeze, the group fancied itself to be a liberator of the people and had already assassinated Oakland School Superintendent Marcus Foster for introducing identification cards into Oakland schools. Patricia Hearst was held in isolation by the group and, by her later account, was subjected to a form of brainwashing, because by April 15, she was photographed wielding an assault rifle and helping in a San Francisco bank robbery. From then until her arrest in September 1975, she identified herself as Tania and as a member of the S.L.A.

On May 17, 1974, the LAPD tracked the gang down to an apartment on East 54th Street in Compton using a number of unpaid parking tickets. A fierce gun battle ensued while the world watched live. Six members of the gang were killed, including DeFreeze, but though at first it was feared that Hearst had been in the house, she and two other members were actually watching the live telecast from Anaheim.

Although she claimed to be a victim of brainwashing, Patty Hearst was tried and convicted of armed robbery and given the maximum sentence of 25 years, plus 10 years for use of a firearm in the commission of a robbery. After less than two years, her sentence was commuted by President Jimmy Carter, and she was released under strict parole conditions. She was granted a full pardon by President Bill Clinton on January 20, 2001—the last day of his presidency.

LAST POLITICAL TIDBITS

Not a Stellar Political Moment

California's Proposition 187 on the 1994 ballot was one of the most controversial of recent years. It was designed to deprive illegal immigrants of health care, public education and other services. It was approved by 58.8 percent of the voters but was later struck down by the courts as unconstitutional. Governor Pete Wilson supported it, and some believe that the rift created between the Republicans and the growing Latino population of California continues to this day.

Really Republican

In the period between 1899 and 1939, the governor's office was a Republican stronghold. Democrat Culbert Lew Olson broke their winning streak in the election of 1938, but he would only stay in office one term. He lost to Republican Earl Warren in 1942, later chief justice of the Supreme Court.

Unpave L.A.

That's the name of one of several environmental groups concerned with restoring the Los Angeles River. As it is now, the river is almost entirely penned into a concrete channel that is sometimes dry enough to film movie car chases and shootouts. However, at one time, it was an unhampered, alluvial river that ran freely over the Los Angeles flood plain. Environmentalists are working on a master plan that would turn the river into "the front door to the city," with a wildlife corridor along its edges instead of the ugly, mostly forgotten thing that it is today.

MURALS

Art for the People

Some of the most vibrant examples of art in Southern California are its murals. Although the first mural in Los Angeles was Juan Antonio's *Fourteen Stations of the Cross*, painted in 1806 at the San Fernando Mission, murals had a more recent renaissance in the 1960s, when they became an important part of telling the tales of Chicano activism.

The Murals of Estrada Courts

Estrada Courts is a low-income housing project that was constructed in 1942–43 during a World War II housing shortage. In the 1970s, it was given a new vibrancy by the Estrada Courts Mural Project, when artists came to paint the life of the barrio and Chicano culture on the large, empty walls on the ends of the buildings.

El Corrido de (or Ballad of) Boyle Heights
On an unpretentious brick wall of a Payless Shoesource in East Los Angeles, a series of panels portray the dynamism of daily life expressed in music and dancing in the Boyle Heights community.

The Fairfax Community Mural

It isn't just the Hispanic community that has expressed its identity through mural art. Created in 1985 by a collaboration of seniors and youth, this black and white mural in the Fairfax district of L.A. depicts the history of Los Angeles Jews, as taken from old photos.

The Great Wall of Los Angeles

This mural in the Tujunga Wash flood control channel is, at 2754 feet, reputed to be the longest mural in the world. It was conceived by artist Judy Baca as a representation of the diverse peoples of California from prehistory to the 1950s. Over 400 people were involved in the completion of this project, which began in 1974 and finished in 1983.

Farmer John's Pig Mural

Not all mural art is political in nature. In 1957, Francis and Bernard Clougherty, founders of the Farmer John meat brand, commissioned movie scene painter Les Grimes to beautify their factory in the industrial town of Vernon with a mural—a pig mural. It covers an entire city block, and it is probably one of the funnier murals in L.A.'s rich tradition because it shows hundreds of pigs gamboling in what is a very industrial part of L.A. Perhaps it is also one of the more macabre ones; the building it festoons is actually a meat-packing plant. When he was done with the first picture, Les kept on painting, right on up to his death in 1968. Arno Jordan carried on his work, while also restoring some of the older murals.

Unbridled

On Ocean Park Boulevard at 4th Street in Santa Monica, this fanciful 25-by-600-foot mural by David Gordon features carousel horses escaping from the Santa Monica Pier carousel and running along the beach.

Whale of a Mural

Across the street on the other side of the underpass stretches a large work by Daniel Alonzo. Of the same dimensions as Gordon's, this one depicts cavorting whales and other playful ocean creatures.

ARTISTIC TEMPERAMENT

She Shocked Herself
(and probably a lot of other people, too)

Ojai is an artists' colony par excellence, and there's no better example of the type of artist who came to settle there than ceramist Beatrice Wood, who dominated the local art scene for decades. A San Francisco society girl who decided to become an artist rather than a debutante, she led a wild life that took her through several continents and into arms of Marcel Duchamp and the Dadaists, among others. Having burnt through more careers than most of us could achieve in several lifetimes, she didn't take her first ceramics class until she arrived in Los Angeles in her forties. But by the time she settled in Ojai in 1948, she was already a renowned ceramist. She even started a new career as writer while in her late eighties. It was none other than famed diarist Anais Nin who encouraged her to write her autobiography, *I Shock Myself.* She apparently had plenty of time to take up that new pursuit; she didn't shuffle off these mortal coils until 1998, at the ripe old age of 105. Some of her work is in the permanent collection at the Beatrice Wood Center for the Arts, which also holds exhibitions, workshops and performances.

DID YOU  **KNOW?**

When asked what the key to her longevity was, Wood answered, "Art books, chocolates and young men." Now that sounds like a health regime I could follow.

MUSIC

Let's Go Surfin' Now

Dick Dale (born Richard Monsour), "King of the Surf Guitar," is often credited with writing the first real surf rock song, "Let's Go Trippin'"(1961). He also introduced the guitar "reverb" (a reverberating effect created by electronic means), which gives surf music its classic "wet" sound. A true surfer, Dale wanted his music to express the sounds that came to his mind while surfing.

The Landlubbers?

In contrast, The Beach Boys were not surfers. Of the five original members, brothers Brian, Carl and Dennis, cousin Mike Love and friend Alan Jardine, only Dennis Wilson was actually a surfer. However, he convinced the others to make music about that lifestyle, and, boy, was that the right decision. Writing about surfing, girls and cars led the group to 36 U.S. Top 40 hits, including four number one singles: "I Get Around" (1964), "Help Me, Rhonda" (1965), "Good Vibrations" (1966) and the later "Kokomo" (1988).

DID YOU KNOW?

Singer Glen Campbell was a replacement member of The Beach Boys for several months after Brian Wilson suffered a breakdown while on tour in December 1964. Campbell originally came out to Los Angeles as a session musician and became part of an acclaimed group known as The Wrecking Crew. Almost infinitely versatile, they backed up everyone from Bing Crosby to, yes, The Beach Boys.

Trippin' for Real

In the late 1960s and early '70s, Sunset Strip, the portion of Sunset Boulevard that runs through West Hollywood, became a major center of the counterculture. Clubs such as Whisky a Go Go, The Roxy and The London Fog served as venues for bands such as The Byrds, The Doors and Buffalo Springfield. Although diverse in other ways, these bands can be lumped under the heading Psychedelic Rock; in that era, most of them were heavily partaking of mind-altering substances. The Byrds released "Eight Mile High" in December 1965, considered by many to be the first fully psychedelic recording. The lyrics have to do with an airplane trip, but they were easily read as being about a drug trip. And Jim Morrison made The Doors' first (live) appearance on *The Ed Sullivan Show* their last when he "forgot" to change the lyrics of "Light My Fire" from "Girl, we couldn't get much higher" to "Girl, we couldn't get much better," as he was supposed to have done. Needless to say, Sullivan was furious.

Not to be left out, San Diego also contributed a famous psychedelic band—Iron Butterfly, perhaps best known for their single "In-a-Gadda-Da-Vida" (1968).

Sea Shanties?

Musical innovators Frank Zappa and Captain Beefheart, a.k.a. Don Van Vliet, both spent their teenage years in Antelope Valley, in the Mojave Desert, where they became friends and collaborators. In 1969, Zappa produced his friend's *Trout Mask Replica*, a double album that was inspired by jazz, blues and other forms of American music, including the work of Bo Diddly, and yes, sea shanties. It is widely considered a groundbreaking masterpiece and is No. 58 on *Rolling Stone's* list of the 500 Greatest Albums of All Time.

Not Just the Father of Moon Unit

Zappa is, of course, a legend in his own right. In his 30-year career, cut short by prostate cancer, he contributed to a wide array of musical styles including rock, jazz, doo-wop, blues and classical music. He was one of the most prolific musician/composers of his era, releasing over 60 albums during his lifetime, most of which consisted of his own compositions. As gifted in the recording studio as he was at his music, after 1966, he also produced just about every recording he made himself. In fact, he increasingly blended these two gifts, using tape editing as a compositional tool in its own right, and finding ways to add live guitar solos to the final studio recordings of a work.

Frank Zappa ran afoul of the law once in the early 1960s when his fledgling recording company, Studio Z in Rancho Cucamonga, agreed to make a sound-only sex tape for a stag party for $100. He and a female friend made it as a joke, editing out the laughs. Unfortunately, the stag party was really a cover for the vice squad, and Zappa ended up spending 10 days in jail for supplying pornography. Suffice it to say that entrapment and imprisonment did nothing to improve his anti-authoritarian stance.

Valley Vernacular

In 1982, Frank Zappa released the album *Ship Arriving Too Late to Save a Drowning Witch*. On it was a song called "Valley Girl," sung by his daughter, Moon Unit Zappa, which contained phrases of valley girl slang—that is, the vernacular of a girl from the well-to-do classes of San Fernando Valley. Although Zappa intended it as a satire of what he considered their vapid-sounding speech, the song had the opposite effect, and soon "Valspeak" was being spoken nationwide.

Funk and Fusion

The late 1960s and early 1970s saw country music and rock fusing in Los Angeles groups such as The Eagles and Poco. This was also when War, still one of the most enduring funk groups, came into existence in South L.A. War was a multiracial group blending many musical styles. Despite the name, the group was trying to spread a message of peace and harmony during the era of the Vietnam War. Perhaps their half-satirical, half-sincere 1975 song "Why Can't We Be Friends?" expresses what they meant a little better than their name did.

Feeling Kind of Punk

Punk rock had its day in Southern California, even though it never made the headlines in the same way as its counterparts in London or New York. But groups such as The Germs, who are usually thought to have recorded the first punk record of Los Angeles with *Forming/Sexyboy* (live), and The Screamers had their fan bases. And hardcore punk groups, which emerged in the late 1970s with a heavier sound than early punk bands, definitely had some roots in Southern California—the Orange County group Middle Class is considered by some to be the first hardcore punk band in the world, though it vies with groups like Black Flag and Bad Brains for the title. A San Diego band called Unbroken became quite influential throughout California, and the San Fernando Valley contributed the group Bad Religion, whose lyrics spoke of both political and personal responsibility. In the 1980s, a further fusion would bring about "skacore," which was a blend of punk hardcore and Jamaican-influenced ska.

Let's Get Rid of L.A.
No, not really. It just happens to be the name of the album that brought 16 L.A. punk bands to the attention of the city and perhaps the world. No one is sure if it helped or hurt that the album included a 44-page manifesto/band historiography. One critic describes the album as "L.A. giving itself a good talking to." Which heaven knows it needs sometimes.

Glam 'n' Grit

Heavy metal found a new voice on the Sunset Strip in the early 1980s, specifically in the sub-genre known as glam rock or, more mockingly, hair rock, after the musicians' flowing hairstyles that were often their trademark. Groups such as Quiet Riot, formed in 1975, and Mötley Crüe, which was formed in 1981 and went on to become one of the most famous heavy metal bands of all time, led the way. In the late '80s, groups such as Poison, which was actually a transplant from Pennsylvania, and Guns N' Roses, a true Los Angeles product, came along and replaced the glam rock bands with a grittier hard rock sound.

How California Came to Hip Hop

Hip hop, invented in New York but with roots in the musical rhythms of Africa and Jamaica, certainly made a long journey west. But when it got to L.A., it wasn't tired at all. Instead it developed a new distinctive style, and West Coast hip hop was born, sending its own big stars back to the nation in return. Even people far from this particular musical scene have heard the names of Ice-T, who some say brought out the first gangsta rap track in the mid-1980s; Dr. Dre, who collaborated with Easy-E and Ice Cube on the genre-defining album *Straight Outta Compton* under the name N.W.A.; and Snoop Doggy Dogg, now Snoop Dogg, who has gone on to win numerous music awards and has been nominated for multiple Grammys.

How 'bout We Take It on the Road?

The Dorothy Chandler Music Pavilion houses the world-class Los Angeles Opera Company. Its debut was in 1986, but it traces its roots back to the Los Angeles Civic Grand Opera, which started in 1948. Its artistic director is currently the great Spanish tenor Placido Domingo, and its music director is James Conlon. However, the opera will be homeless in 2011 while the Pavilion undergoes renovations, and among the options being considered, Placido Domingo has said that the company might tour Japan.

 The San Diego Opera is nothing to laugh at either, having been ranked by Opera America as one of the top 10 opera companies in the United States.

A Bowlful of Trivia

On July 11, 1922, the first season of the Hollywood Bowl was inaugurated with Alfred Hertz leading the Los Angeles Philharmonic, while the audience sat on wooden benches climbing the bowl-shaped sides of Bolton Canyon. The Bowl is one of the largest natural amphitheaters in the world, with a seating capacity of just under 18,000. It's been the summer home of the Los Angeles Philharmonic from the beginning, and since 1991 has also had a resident ensemble, the Hollywood Bowl Orchestra. Only a handful of concerts have ever had to be cancelled because of rain. Individual concert tickets cost less than 50 cents during the early days, and even now, one dollar will buy you a seat at the top of the Bowl for many of the concerts.

If you can think of a legendary performer from the last 50 years, particularly a musical one, chances are they've been on stage at the Bowl. Frank Sinatra, Ella Fitzgerald, the Beatles, Simon and Garfunkel, Nureyev and even Abbott and Costello have graced this stage. But the all-time attendance record of 26,410 paid admissions was set on August 7, 1936, by French opera star Lily Pons.

There are three statues in the fountain at the Highland entrance to the Bowl, representing the muses of Music, Dance and Drama. They were designed by George Stanley, the man who sculpted the prototype for some of the most famed statuettes in the history of the world—the Oscar statuettes.

ARCHITECTURE

How the Space Age Came to LAX

The Theme Building is certainly an iconic landmark of Los Angeles International Airport. It looks like a landed spaceship, with a restaurant suspended in air between four intersecting legs. Built in 1961, it is space age as only buildings of the 1960s can be. *The Jetsons* cartoon was visualized on its lines, and in a nice twist, Walt Disney Imagineering redesigned what came to be the Encounter Restaurant to look like something out of *The Jetsons*. A team of architectural firms was responsible for the building: Pereira and Luckman, Welton Becket and Associates and Paul R. Williams Associated Architects.

DID YOU  **KNOW?**

Paul R. Williams, who took part in the design and construction of the Theme Building, was the first certified African-American architect west of the Mississippi. Sometimes referred to as "the architect to the stars," he designed over 2000 private homes, many of them in the Hollywood Hills. His most famous homes were built for celebrities like Frank Sinatra, Lucille Ball and Danny Thomas. The irony was not lost on him that most of the homes he designed and whose construction he supervised were built on tracts of land with deeds containing segregation covenants that banned African Americans from buying them.

House of Glass

In Garden Grove, you can visit the amazing Crystal Cathedral, which rises in the shape of a four-pointed star to a height of 124 feet. Dedicated by founding minister Robert Schulyer in September 1980, the cathedral has over 10,000 panes of reflective glass. They are designed to allow only eight percent of outside light in, giving the interior an underwater feeling. The supporting structure is an incredibly delicate framework of steel tubing, which in effect works much like a giant chimney, allowing heat to rise out of the building and thus preventing a greenhouse effect. The building can house nearly 3000 people, but if you get there late for service, don't worry—you can join the cars that assemble in the parking lot every Sunday for drive-in services. The architect of this marvel was Philip Johnson.

DID YOU  KNOW?

The Crystal Cathedral houses one of the largest organs in the world, and certainly one that has been seen by more people than most—the Crystal Cathedral broadcasts its services around the world. Named the Hazel Wright Pipe Organ in honor of its donor (who gave more than $2 million for it), it was designed especially for the glass cathedral by organ virtuoso Virgil Fox, who combined two instruments—the Aeolian-Skinner instrument from New York's Lincoln Center and the Ruffati organ from Neutra Sanctuary. It now has 270 ranks, 31 digital ranks and 16,000 pipes! Its 14 divisions can be played from two five-manual consoles.

They Don't Make 'em Like This Anymore

The oldest commercial building still standing in the center of downtown Los Angeles, the Bradbury Building was commissioned by mining tycoon Louis Bradbury and built between 1889 and 1893. The central courtyard is five stories tall and is capped by a skylight, which allows natural light into the building at all times of day. The materials used in the courtyard are glazed brick, polished wood, French wrought iron, Mexican tile and Belgian marble. The ornate iron grillwork is meant to suggest hanging vegetation. It is still a matter of speculation whether Sumner Hunt, who turned in initial designs, or George H. Wyman, who supervised the project, is the ultimate genius behind this masterpiece. Fortunately for future generations, the building was renovated and seismically retrofitted in 1991.

You may not have visited the Bradbury Building yet, but chances are you've seen it. It has provided the setting for many major films, most famously *Blade Runner*, but also *Chinatown, Double Indemnity* and *D.O.A.*

Gehry and Disney—Together at Last

The Walt Disney Concert Hall is the newest addition to the Los Angeles Music Center in downtown Los Angeles. Designed by world-class but controversial artist Frank Gehry, it opened on October 23, 2003. Launched by Walt Disney's widow, Lilian, with a donation of $50 million, and with Gehry's plans handed in in 1991, the project still managed to languish for a while because of a lack of funds. When plans were revised and much less expensive metal skin replaced the costly stone exterior, things proceeded apace again. Although the playful unpredictability of the building, like all Gehry's work, plays better to some groups than to others (the façade of the organ within, which Gehry also designed, was said to resemble a bag of french fries by one critic), all seem to agree that it is acoustically superior to its predecessor, the neighboring Dorothy Chandler Pavilion.

DID YOU  KNOW?

Although the metal cladding that ended up sheathing the Concert Hall was less costly, it did take its toll—on the neighbors. The surface acted like a parabolic mirror in its ability to concentrate and reflect glare, causing some neighboring condominiums to heat up to unbearable temperatures, and creating hot spots on nearby sidewalks that reached 140°F! Ticket booth workers reported seeing traffic cones melt and trash cans self-combust. After a computer analysis was done on the building in 2005, the trouble spots on the building were identified and sanded to reduce the glare.

Getty Old, Getty New— but Which is Which?

Getty Center is the current home of the J. Paul Getty Museum. It opened on December 16, 1997. Sitting on the hillside above the 405 Freeway, and made out of white travertine, it's a hard-to-miss presence. After parking at the base of the hill, visitors ascend via tram to the Arrival Plaza and then continue on foot up to the Entrance Hall, which is a series of five pavilions connected by glass walkways.

After a nine-year renovation, the Getty Villa in Malibu finally reopened its doors in 2006, though not until $276 million had been shelled out (not a problem, though—the J. Paul Getty Trust, with over $3 billion to spend, has the largest art endowment in history). The building was built in 1974, modeled after the first-century Roman Villa dei Papiri, which was buried when Mt. Vesuvius erupted. Getty wanted people to experience what it was like to be in a Mediterranean Villa, and the renovation added more light and expanded tiny rooms, which can only help the country's only museum devoted entirely to antiquities. Too bad Getty did not live to see the re-creation himself.

DID YOU  **KNOW?**

The chapel at San Juan Capistrano is the oldest building still in use in California, and it is the only surviving church of those used by Father Junipero Serra.

Red Tile Tour

Santa Barbara has its own unique architectural style, which, though it appears at first glance to be from the Mission era, is actually a fantastical reimagining of old mission days. The city that was devastated in the 1925 earthquake was a much more conventional California town of the era, and it was only in rebuilding that Bernhard Hoffman, founder of the City Planning Commission, decided to try to recapture some of the early Spanish-Mexican flavor. But Santa Barbara architecture is a blend of several styles, including the Moorish and Mediterranean. Its main elements are the famous red tile roofs, white walls, courtyards and the wrought iron that is used ornamentally in windows, staircases and other features. The style is enforced by strict city ordinances.

The Stingaree

The Gaslamp Quarter is a historic district of downtown San Diego that contains 94 historic buildings in a 16-and-a-half-block area. There are four new gas lamps to represent the older lamps that once lined the street. Many of the buildings are still in use by tenants today. This quarter was at one time called the "Stingaree" and was San Diego's red light district, being the home of many undesirables such as prostitutes, pimps, gamblers and drug dealers. Here are some highlights:

☛ The William Heath Davis house is the oldest surviving wooden structure in the downtown area. It is a "salt box" style of construction from 1850 and is actually an early version of a "pre-fab" home. It was framed on the East Coast and then shipped all the way around Cape Horn to San Diego.

☛ The building that housed the Royal Pie bakery still stands. There was a bakery on this site from 1871 to 1996. Even when it became enveloped in the red-light district, it kept on plying its wares—just as the notorious brothel upstairs plied its own.

☛ The McGurck Block, 1887, is a three-story Italianate Revival building. It once housed the Ferris and Ferris Drugstore, at that time San Diego's only all-night drugstore. Gregory Peck's father once worked there as the night druggist. It has also been a post office and a ticket office for the Coronado Ferry. It now houses Z Galleries, which bought the crumbling building from the San Diego Historical Society for one dollar and opened a store in the fully renovated building in 1996. It has since won numerous awards, which makes me proud to be the president of the company's sister-in-law.

☛ In Horton Plaza Park lies a fountain by local architect Irving Gill. It is based upon the choragic monument of

Lysicrates in Athens. Inscribed in 1909 and dedicated in 1910, it was the first successful attempt to combine colored lights and flowing water.

☛ The two-towered Louis Bank of Commerce is a landmark of the Gaslamp Quarter. It was built in 1888 and was the first building in San Diego to be made of granite. It was once home to a 24-hour ice cream parlor, an oyster bar that famed lawman Wyatt Earp was partial to and, perhaps inevitably, a brothel.

☛ In Horton Plaza, you can find the 1906 Jessop Street Clock, which has 20 dials, 12 of which are dedicated to telling the time around the world. The clock was designed by Joseph Jessop Sr. to stand outside his jewelry shop, but it was actually built mainly by Charles D. Ledger, a graduate of the Elgin Watch School. When the clock was completed in 1907, it was entered in the Sacramento State Fair, where it won a gold medal for its movement. The clock's trip to Sacramento brought it an extra passenger. A child had attached a tiny carved bear to the pendulum by means of a ring, and when this proved impossible to remove, the bear was destined to ride the pendulum forever. It can still be seen today.

DID YOU KNOW?

Understandably, Charles Ledger was always very fussy about the clock, never letting anyone else touch it. Word has it that when Ledger died in 1935, the clock stopped. It was restarted, but it stopped again three days later—on the day of Ledger's funeral.

The Talk of the Western World

The Hotel Del Coronado lies on the San Diego Bay on a peninsula so isolated that it is almost an island. Elisha Babcock purchased 4100 acres of windy, unproductive land in 1888 with the dream of building a hotel that would be "the talk of the western world." And he succeeded in doing just that. From the beginning, the massive, red-roofed Victorian building has drawn celebrities and dignitaries of all stripes. Ten U.S. presidents have visited "the Del," starting with Benjamin Harrison in 1891. Charles Lindbergh was honored there after his historic trans-Atlantic flight in 1927, and at the dinner, a replica of *The Spirit of St. Louis* circled the crown room ceiling. Frank L. Baum, Thomas Edison and Babe Ruth have all been guests. So have Madonna and Brad Pitt.

The Hotel Del Coronado was the backdrop for the 1958 Hollywood classic *Some Like it Hot*, starring Marilyn Monroe, Jack Lemmon and Tony Curtis.

DID YOU  KNOW?

The Prince of Wales, later King Edward VIII, was a guest at the Del in 1920. He famously abdicated the throne for Wallis Simpson, a Coronado divorcée. Speculation is rife that he first met her at the hotel.

LITERATURE

Maybe Beach Reading is Underrated

Although Southern California may have a certain reputation for airheadedness, statistics put the lie to stereotypes. Los Angeles County is the largest book market in the country. According to the U.S. Census Bureau report of 1997, although the population of L.A. County exceeds that of the New York greater metropolitan area by six percent, it spends a whopping 37 percent more on books!

From Masters of Literature to Hollywood Hacks!

More than one famous writer has come to Hollywood to try his or her luck at the screenplay trade, and some of them have then recycled their often bitter experiences back into good novels.

Christopher Isherwood, who wrote *The Berlin Stories*, which are famously the source for the musical *Cabaret*, did a stint in Hollywood and then wrote a novel about a young man hired to write a screenplay in *Prater Violet*.

F. Scott Fitzgerald portrayed his own experience as a hack writer at the studios in *The Pat Hobby Stories*, about a down-and-out screenwriter looking for a break who gets tragically involved with a younger woman.

Even John O'Hara got into the act with his own washed up screenwriter story, *Hope of Heaven*.

William Faulkner was another novelist who went to Hollywood hoping that screenwriting would pay the bills. Two of his most successful adaptations were of *The Big Sleep*, by Raymond Chandler, and *To Have and Have Not*, by Ernest Hemingway. Not to shabby, Bill.

A British View

Maybe satire is the best way to write about Los Angeles—
Evelyn Waugh certainly thought so, anyway. *The Loved One* is
his parody of the Los Angeles funeral industry, and much of the
action centers around Whispering Glades, a thinly disguised
Forest Lawn, where the stars—and their pets—go to be buried.

The Slumming Angel

Raymond Chandler brought the crime novel to a new literary
level when he introduced the private investigator Philip Marlowe
in his 1939 novel, *The Big Sleep*. Beyond just creating a new
archetype of the wisecracking P.I. with his own invincible code
of honor, Chandler had also found a way to talk about Los
Angeles and its neighboring cities, capturing their ambience,
natural beauty and the corruption that lies in the shadows. He
had reason to know a little about that—before returning late in
life to his early dreams of being a writer, he had spent a period
working for an oil company where, despite his dislike for it, he
rose to the position of vice president.

Chandleresque

A whole school of writers have followed in Chandler's footsteps, and some of the best write about Southern California:

☛ Ross MacDonald, pen name for Kenneth Miller, took up Chandler's mantel when he began writing the Lew Archer novels. The Moving Target, published in 1949, was set in fictional Santa Teresa, a thinly veiled Santa Barbara.

☛ These days, Sue Grafton has moved her own female detective, Kinsey Milhone, into the Santa Teresa community.

☛ The current crop of crime writers includes Michael Connelly and his Hieronymus "Harry" Bosch series, which often portrays the LAPD detective's protective love of his city and disenchantment with its policing.

☛ T. Jefferson Parker's novels contrast the sunny climate with the dark crimes committed in Southern California.

☛ Walter Mosley has long used the hardboiled genre to tackle issues of race in Southern California. His Easy Rollins series features a black detective who has to deal with issues of race and gender in post–World War II Southern California. Mosley isn't one to be pigeonholed, though— he's written everything from political books to what some call "Afro-futurist" science fiction.

DID YOU KNOW?

James Ellroy's impetus for writing in the noir style that brought us such books as *The Black Dahlia* and *L.A. Confidential* is a little different than most. In 1958, when he was just 10 years old, his mother was murdered. She had just divorced his father and relocated to Los Angeles with James. Her murder remains unsolved, and Ellroy began *My Dark Places*, a book about her death and about his own unresolved feelings, when friend and reporter Frank Giradot gained access to some LAPD police files on the murder.

Apocalypse How?

When not puncturing Southern California boosters' pretensions to live in the best of all possible worlds, or casting it in a noir light, California writers still often visit the dark side by giving their stories an apocalyptic cast. You can hardly blame them—there are so many disastrous scenarios to choose from:

☛ Nathanael West's *The Day of the Locust* ends with an apocalyptic mob riot outside a Hollywood premiere.

☛ In Carolyn See's *Golden Days,* the narrator chronicles her days in Malibu leading up to and following a nuclear holocaust.

☛ In *This Book Will Save Your Life* by A.M. Homes, the city of L.A. collapses around the protagonist's eyes.

☛ *The Tortilla Curtain*, T.C. Boyle's novel of cultural clashes and miscommunication in and around Topanga Canyon, comes to an end in the twin disasters of fire and mud.

The Case of the Prolific Novelist

One of the most successful writers of modern times lived in Temecula and practiced law in Oxnard and Ventura. Erle Stanley Gardner began writing stories for the pulp magazines until he hit upon his most lasting character: Perry Mason.

Viva El Pachuco!

Zoot Suit was written by Luis Valdez and perfected in the collective theater works company, El Teatro Campesino, whose home base is in San Juan Bautista. The play was first performed in Los Angeles in 1978 and later went to Broadway, as well as being made into a film. It is a drama that centers on the real life Sleepy Lagoon murder trial of a group of pachucos and the Zoot Suit Riots of 1943, when military men of all stripes descended upon East Los Angeles and attacked every man wearing a flashy zoot suit. In the play, the mythical figure of El Pachuco communes with the main character, Henry Rayna, acting as interpreter to the action and embodying all the pride, defiance and coolness to which the Zoot Suiters aspired. In the play's cathartic moment, El Pachuco shares the fate of the Zoot Suiters and is stripped of his suit, but rises again as an Aztec god.

NEWS MEDIA

Just the Facts, Ma'am

The Los Angeles Times is the largest daily paper in the county and actually the second largest metropolitan newspaper in the U.S., after *The New York Times*. When its last main rival, *The Herald-Express*, went out of business in 1989, L.A. became in effect a one-newspaper city. However, adjoining communities such as the San Fernando Valley and Orange County have their own papers that compete with *The Times* within their own regions.

The Facts *en Español*

La Opinión is the city's major Spanish-language newspaper, and the largest Spanish-language paper in the United States. It was founded on September 16, 1926, to coincide with Mexican Independence Day. Although its early function was mainly to provide news from home for the large Los Angeles immigrant community, these days it covers issues of interest to a much more diverse Spanish-speaking community. In the words of its former publisher, Ignacio E. Lozano Jr., "Our mission was no longer to be a Mexican newspaper published in Los Angeles, but an American newspaper that happened to be written in Spanish."

FILM AND TELEVISION

Homegrown

☛ Child star Shirley Temple, later Shirley Temple Black, was born in Santa Monica. So was Robert Redford.

☛ Gregory Peck, then known as Eldred Gregory Peck, was born in La Jolla, outside San Diego. So was Robert Duvall.

☛ Marilyn Monroe, also known as Norma Jeane Mortenson, was born in the Los Angeles County Hospital.

☛ Kevin Costner came into the world in Linwood, in the southern part of the L.A. Basin.

☛ Dustin Hoffman was born in Los Angeles.

☛ Gene Hackman was born in San Bernardino.

☛ Drew Barrymore was born in Culver City.

On the Street Where You Live

One of the most densely populated of star-studded streets is Roxbury Drive in Beverly Hills. This single street has housed some of the biggest celebrities, both past and present. Jimmy Stewart lived here, as did Jack Benny and Lucille Ball. Ricky Shroeder, child television star, lived here once, as did other popular television actors such as Elizabeth Montgomery of *Bewitched* and Peter Falk of *Columbo*.

Studying the Studios

There was a Universal Studios tour even in the silent picture days, but it was a far cry from what the tour has become. Back then, you could buy produce because the studio still showed traces of the chicken farm it had been when Carl Laemmle bought it in 1912 and turned it into a production lot. Over the years, Universal Studios has grown into a colossus, with 36 sound stages and employing 10,000 artists. The Universal Tour has grown into something unrecognizable too, with movie-themed thrill rides and stunts far overshadowing the humble back-lot tour that is still part of the tram ride. If you're ready to shell out, you can go on a 15-person private tour, which allows you to see the costume and production shops and a bit of the sound stage, as well as jump the long lines for those rides, of course.

If the mere sound of this half-day extravaganza leaves you feeling exhausted, you could always try the NBC Studio Tour, which is only 70 minutes long and actually takes you behind the scenes of a major television network, where you'll get to walk on the set of *The Tonight Show with Jay Leno* and see all the production shops as well.

Warner Brothers Studios also has a tour that takes you behind the scenes of a vast multimedia empire. There's even a museum where, among much other memorabilia from the studio's long history, you can see the Oscar that the studio got for the first talkie, *The Jazz Singer*.

Ceremonious Oscar Trivia

☛ The Hollywood Roosevelt Hotel hosted the first awards ceremony in 1929. There was dinner and dancing.

☛ The first Academy Awards ceremony was also the shortest. The acceptance speech portion lasted only 15 minutes, partly because the awards had been announced three months earlier.

☛ The longest awards ceremony was held in 2002 and lasted 256 minutes. I suppose that's when organizers got serious about drowning out the acceptance speeches with music when winners had run past their allotted time.

☛ Elizabeth Taylor once threw a loser's party at the Polo Lounge on Sunset Boulevard to celebrate all those to whom "it was an honor just to be nominated."

☛ The Kodak Theatre is the site of the actual awards ceremony these days, with the Governor's Ball being thrown on the rooftops of the giant mall complex at Hollywood and Highland. Naturally, fans are out in full force that night on Hollywood Boulevard.

☛ For a while in the 1960s, the Oscars were held in the Santa Monica Civic Auditorium. It was from there that they were first broadcast in color, in 1966.

STANLEY

☛ The Technical Oscars are awarded at the Beverly Wilshire Hotel. This ceremony may not be as exciting as being at the Kodak Theatre on the big night, but the techies have been given a consolation prize in having some hot young actress such as Scarlett Johansson or Maggie Gyllenhaal to host the event.

☛ The Oscar statuette weighs 6.75 pounds and is 13.5 inches high. The Academy librarian, Margaret Herrick, is said to have named it when, upon seeing it, she exclaimed, "Why, that looks like my Uncle Oscar!" He must have been rather short.

☛ In the early days, the awards ceremony was pretty casual because by the time it happened, everyone already knew who had won. The sealed envelope system was not introduced until 1941, which must have raised the tension in the room that year considerably.

☛ The Golden Raspberry Awards ("Razzies") were thought up in 1980 by John Wilson and are linked to the Oscars in their own mirror image sort of way. They "dishonor" the worst acting, directing, choreography, songwriting and films that the industry has to offer. Typically, the awards are announced one day before the Oscars.

DID YOU KNOW?

A Razzie is not usually accepted in person, but a handful of recipients have been man—or woman—enough to make an appearance. Bill Cosby was the first person to accept a Razzie in person. My personal favorite, though, is Tom Green, who has accepted all five of his Razzies and showed up for *Freddy Got Fingered* in a white Cadillac, bearing his own length of red carpet. In his speech he said, "I want to say I didn't deserve this…dear god, I want to say that." He concluded his speech with a never-ending harmonica number, and organizers finally had to drag him off the stage.

INCREDIBLE INVENTIONS

Patently So

☛ UCLA was the place the nicotine patch was invented. UCLA also developed a treatment for intracranial aneurysms.

☛ UC San Diego patented a therapy on treating interstitial cystitis, a painful bladder disease.

☛ UC Santa Barbara developed a pump that measures and delivers insulin to diabetics.

☛ UC Irvine is responsible for inventing a skin-cooling device that helps with laser treatments.

☛ CalTech's Jet Propulsion Laboratory has patented an improved global positioning system and pixel sensor technology for digital cameras.

☛ CalTech has also contributed the DNA sequencer and an ultra-strong "liquid metal."

☛ Work on a chemistry technique called olefin metathesis, which makes it easier and cheaper to create synthetic substances while reducing the amount of waste left over, won CalTech professor Bob Grubb a share in the 2005 Nobel Prize in Chemistry.

☛ USC's Institute for Creative Technology's work in war game training for the army eventually led to an at least theoretically more benign purpose—the popular video game, *Full Spectrum Warrior*.

☛ USC also developed Light Stage 2 technology, now used in big movies like *Spiderman* to realistically record an actor's face for use in special-effect scenes (I suppose so that the actors don't have to really stop full commuter trains on their own, for example).

 The University of California, CalTech and Stanford ranked first, second and fourth in the federal government's list of universities receiving patents in 2005. The combined campuses of the UC system have held the top spot for 12 unbroken years.

Not the *Peace* Prize, You Understand

Glenn Seaborg, who worked on the Manhattan Project (the project that eventually led to the first atomic bomb) and won a Nobel Prize in 1951 for "discoveries in the chemistry of the transuranium elements," grew up in a community that later became part of South Gate.

Gentlemen Prefer Rubies

Los Angeles native Theodore Harold Maiman invented the world's first operable laser in 1960, using a pink ruby medium. He was employed as a section head at Hughes Research Laboratories at the time. Maiman was inducted into the National Inventors Hall of Fame in 1984.

I Know This Will Mean Something to *You...*

Another National Inventors Hall of Fame inductee (1997) was Robert Bower. Born in Santa Monica, Bower invented the Self-Aligned Gate MOSFET in 1965, which made possible the design-stable device that is the foundation for all modern integrated circuits.

But Not For Inventing Disneyland

In 2000, Walt Disney was inducted into the National Inventors Hall of Fame. He was specifically honored for his invention of the multi-plane camera. The result was better looking, richer animation. In 1937, *Snow White and the Seven Dwarves* was the first full-length animated film to use the camera.

The Great Zamboni

In times gone by, when an ice rink got chipped and nicked, repairing the surface was a complicated process. Workers had to scrape the ice with a tractor, sweep away the shavings, hose the surface down and then wait for the surface to dry. But in 1949, Frank Zamboni, owner of a large ice skating rink in Paramount, figured out how to combine all these tasks into one machine: the Zamboni Ice Resurfacer. This machine—or a newer version of it—is still used all over the world today to clean and polish a chipped, nicked and scarred ice rink into an immediately usable surface in one pass.

DID YOU KNOW?

Olympic figure skater Sonja Henie was really the one responsible for marketing the Zamboni. She saw it in action while practicing at the Paramount Rink and immediately ordered one to take with her on her world tour. Soon the Ice Capades and then other rinks and ice skating groups all wanted one of their very own.

The More We Get Together, the Happier We'll Be...

In June 2006, officials from the University of British Columbia and the University of California announced the completion of a new ultra-high bandwidth connection between the two institutes of research and higher learning. This connection allows the two systems to have their own dedicated superhighway that allows the transfer of enormous streams of data that would overwhelm a conventional internet connection.

SPACE COWGIRL

Ride, Sally Ride

Sally Ride was the first American woman in space. She was born in Los Angeles and did her undergraduate and graduate degrees at Stanford. She was aboard the space shuttle *Challenger* in 1983 and was part of the first crew to use the shuttle's robot arm to deploy and receive a satellite in space. Ride went on a second *Challenger* mission and was training for a third, but the space shuttle exploded just after taking off in 1986. She later served on the committee that investigated that tragic accident.

CALIFORNIA CRIME

Sometimes, Things Actually Do Take a Turn for the Better

According to the COMPSTAT unit of the Los Angeles Police Department, violent crimes and property crimes have been showing a marked decline since the mid-1990s. The year 2006 brought a record low in violent crime, with "only" 29,737 acts of violence, which included 481 homicides and 903 rapes. The crime peak of 1992 had 72,667 recorded acts of violence, which included a mind-boggling 1083 homicides and 1770 rapes. There were 102,297 property crimes, which include burglary, personal theft and auto theft, in 2006, as opposed to 245,129 such crimes in 1992.

When comparing total crime in 2006, Los Angeles had a lower crime index than many other cities, including Boston and San Francisco. Of the country's largest cities, only New York City and San Diego had lower overall crime rates.

It's Not Exactly *West Side Story*

As of 2001, Los Angeles County was home to 152,000 gang members, divided into 1350 gangs. The Crips and the Bloods are but two of the famous (or infamous) gangs of the region, much mythologized in film and song.

The Car's the Thing

It should be no surprise that much of L.A. crime and enforcement would be automobile-related. Car chases, drive-by shootings, car-to-car shootings, hit-and-run accidents and carjackings all feature largely in the Los Angeles crime scene.

DID YOU KNOW?

The murder of Ennis Cosby, son of comedian Bill Cosby, sent shockwaves through the country. On January 16, 1997, he had stopped on Interstate 405 to change a flat tire on his Mercedes when he was accosted by a Ukrainian immigrant named Mikail Markhasev, who demanded money from him and then shot him in the head. Although the evidence against Markhasev proved largely circumstantial, he confessed and was convicted of the crime.

SERIOUS AND SERIOUSLY STRANGE LOCAL LAWS

☛ In Ventura County, cats and dogs are not allowed to have sex without a permit.

☛ It's a crime for dogs to have sex within 500 yards of a church. The penalty? A $500 fine, or six months in jail. Now, how is a dog going to come up with $500? I ask you.

☛ Starting in January 1995, it became illegal to trip horses for entertainment.

☛ It's illegal to curse on a mini-golf course.

☞ Zoot suits are prohibited. Luckily for all concerned, they are now a bit out of fashion.

☞ You may be surprised to learn that it is illegal to set metal balloons afloat in the air. Impossible would be more my word, but go figure.

☞ Procrastinators beware! You may be fined as much as $250 if your Christmas lights are up past February 2. Yes, February—it's not a typo.

☞ It's illegal for anyone under 18 years old to buy wax containers. Apparently this is because they melt and create "a waxy, oily, greasy, slippery, dangerous and unsightly condition." Also, the contents of these containers attract large numbers of noxious flies. Yuck! Rest assured though, the rest of the population can buy a wax container at any time, no matter what kind of littering slobs we are.

☞ In 1930, the city of Ontario passed a law forbidding roosters to crow within the city limits.

☞ In Glendale, theaters can only show horror movies on Monday, Tuesday or Wednesday.

☞ Also in Glendale, it's illegal to jump into a passing car. That's right, you read that right. I said "into."

☞ In Riverside, there's still a law on the books that makes it illegal for two people to kiss unless both people wipe their lips with rose water.

☞ It's also illegal in Riverside to carry your lunch down the street between 11:00AM and 1:00PM. Unless it's already in your belly, I presume?

☞ Long Beach has it all nailed down. Cars are the only things allowed in a garage.

☞ In Pasadena, it is illegal for a secretary to be alone in a room with her boss—which must make taking dictation a little difficult.

☞ In Downey, you not only can't teach an old dog new tricks, you can't take him on the elevator with you—or a young dog either, for that matter.

☞ Cathedral City has a big problem with you riding your bicycle through the Fountain of Life.

☞ It's illegal to drive more than 2000 sheep down Hollywood Boulevard at one time. Oh, those crazy film makers and their casts of thousands!

☞ Los Angeles law forbids catching moths under a street lamp. (But what if they're flying to their doom? Isn't that what's called an intervention?)

☞ Washing two babies in the same tub is forbidden in Los Angeles. Parents of twins, beware.

☞ It's illegal to cry on the witness stand in L.A., too—even after you've been caught washing those two babies.

☞ But, in case you were thinking that Los Angeles was a little, well, invasive domestically, rest assured that it is legally okay for a man to beat his wife with a strap, as long as it's less than two inches wide. Loophole (no pun intended): if she consents to it, it's okay for him to use a wider strap…

☞ Did I forget to mention that in Los Angeles, toads may not be licked?

☞ A 1924 Fullerton law makes it illegal to park your car between 2:00AM and 5:00AM on any street or highway in the city. It is apparently still very much enforced.

☞ No, however much you want to show him off, in Palm Springs, you may not walk your camel down Palm Canyon Drive between 4:00PM and 6:00PM.

- In Redlands, you may not drive a motor vehicle on city streets unless a man with a lantern is walking ahead of it.

- In San Diego, they'd better not catch you shooting jackrabbits from the back of a streetcar.

- Walnut seems to have the other cities beaten when it comes to strict ordinances, though. Ice cream men must obtain a license before selling ice cream from their cars. Okay, well, maybe that one makes sense.

- But what about this Walnut ordinance? Kites may not be flown over 10 feet above the ground. Let's go fly a kite? No—let's not bother.

- Also in Walnut, children may not wear Halloween masks unless they get a special permit from the sheriff.

- The poor Walnut sheriff probably has carpal tunnel by now, because any men wishing to dress as women must obtain a permit from him or her, too.

- Finally, one cannot leave sand in one's own driveway.

MOST DANGEROUS PLACES

Enter at Your Own Risk

In an annual survey released by a private research firm, Compton had the dubious distinction of being the fourth most dangerous city in the United States as of October 2006. And San Bernardino placed 24th in the top 25 most dangerous cities. But on the bright side, six Southern California cities all made it onto the list of the safest places to live: Mission Viejo (3), Irvine (7), Thousand Oaks (11), Simi Valley (17), Lake Forest (15) and Chino Hills (21).

DID YOU KNOW?

Compton is known worldwide as the home of gangsta rap, a style of rap music that finds its themes in the violent lives of inner-city gang members and other criminals. It is also where tennis champions Venus and Serena Williams grew up. If you were thinking these two facts are unrelated, you are probably unaware that the Williams' older sister was shot and killed in Compton on September 14, 2003.

Look Both Ways

More than 20 percent of all traffic fatalities are pedestrians. With over 700 pedestrian deaths and 14,000 injuries in California per year, it might be worthwhile to see how Southern California cities stack up in the bigger picture before you put on those walking shoes. Although Vallejo up north tops the chart when it comes to the Pedestrian Danger Index for cities over 100,000, Inglewood, Oxnard and Oceanside all follow right behind. And Long Beach, at number 10 on the list, has nothing to gloat about. It had 11 fatalities and 322 injuries in 2001.

CALIFORNIA CRIMINALS

I Guess it Depends on Your Perspective...

Two of the most famous criminals in early Southern California history might well have been termed freedom fighters in another place and time. Like many other Mexicans of that era, Joaquin Murrieta and his family came north to get their share of the California Gold Rush but found themselves the victims of discrimination and persecution. Murrieta joined a group of bandits and eventually became their leader. For two years, this group robbed and terrorized California until a deputy sheriff, Captain Harry Love of Los Angeles County, was authorized by the state to hunt down the gang and either kill or capture the men. The gang was captured in July 1853, and Murrieta is believed to have been killed. His head—or certainly someone's—was preserved in alcohol and paraded through the mining camps for identification.

Murrieta's afterlife may be more significant than his actual one. Only a year after his death, a Cherokee author named John Rollin Ridge wrote *The Life and Adventures of Joaquin Murieta: the Celebrated California Bandit.* The book was wildly popular, as were all the subsequent plagiarized versions of it. Whatever the actual truth of his life, his name has become a rallying point for activists opposed to Anglo-American economic and political domination of California.

Tiburcio Vasquez was real enough, though. After stabbing a constable at a party in Monterey at the age of 14, Vasquez took to a life of crime. He was in and out of San Quentin for horse theft, and ended up hiding out in what became known as the Vasquez Rocks at Tejon Pass in Southern California. He eluded the police for months in these tricky rock formations, but in the end he was betrayed by a friend. He was finally captured in May 1874 and eventually ended up in San José for trial. His jail cell proved to be an early tourist attraction, and thousands of people (mainly women) went to see him.

Before his hanging on March 19, 1875, he dictated a statement that may lead one to think his actions were more political than the surface revealed: "A spirit of hatred and revenge took possession of me. I had numerous fights in defense of what I believed to be my rights and those of my countrymen. I believed we were unjustly deprived of the social rights that belonged to us."

At the gallows, he had only one word to say: "Pronto."

The Many Lives of Murph the Surf

Jack Roland Murphy was about as quintessential a Southern California beach boy as you would want to find. Born in Los Angeles in 1938, he became a member of the Pittsburgh Symphony Orchestra at the age of only 15. He went on to become Florida's top surfer in 1962 and 1963.

But his real claim to fame was that he masterminded what is often regarded as the heist of the 20th century. On October 29, 1964, he and his partners in crime broke into New York City's American Museum of Natural History and stole the Star of India sapphire, along with over 20 other gems. Some of these jewels were so famous that they were impossible to sell, making Jack Murphy's success short lived. He and his cohorts were arrested a couple of days later.

Murphy's 21 months in jail apparently did not agree with him, and after his release, his crimes became increasingly more coercive and violent. In 1967, he was arrested and tried for the murder of two California secretaries. In what became known as the Whiskey Creek murders, the two women had been shot, bludgeoned and dumped in a creek in Hollywood, Florida. Murphy was convicted of one of the murders and served the full sentence. He claims to have been converted during his incarceration, and these days, chameleon that he is, he's wearing yet another mantle. You guessed it—he's an evangelical minister. He's still having a hard time shaking the old nickname, though.

Family Values

On August 9, 1969, Charles Manson and the Family shook the world when they committed the gruesome killings in Hollywood that came to be known as the Tate–La Bianca murders. Manson sent members of his quasi-religious cult to a house rented by film director Roman Polanski and his pregnant wife, Sharon Tate, where they murdered Tate and five of her friends, and subsequently murdered three others, including supermarket executive Leno La Bianca and his wife, Rosemary. The world was shocked by both the brutality of the killings and the cultish obedience to Manson shown by his young followers. Although, sadly, we've all grown a bit more familiar with cult behavior since then, these murders showed the world a dark flip side to the "make love not war" credo of the free-thinking 1960s.

Ironically, Manson and cohorts were initially arrested not in relation to these murders, but because they were suspected of vandalizing a part of Death Valley National Park when they were hiding out in the Mojave Desert afterwards.

DID YOU  KNOW?

Doris Day's son, music producer Terry Melcher, once rented the house that Tate and her friends were murdered in. Melcher had refused to produce Manson's songs, and rumor has had it ever since that getting revenge on Melcher was the reason he chose that house. Investigators have discounted this notion, but what remains true is that Melcher has become a part of this sad bit of history, willing or not.

Speaking of crime, the L.A. County Coroner has what I can only assume is a pretty unique gift shop. What would a coroner's office stock in its gift shop? This one, officially called Skeletons in the Closet, has toe-tag key rings and doormats showing the chalk outline of a body and the words "Los Angeles County Coroner" (what would that be called, exactly—an "unwelcome" mat?). Although macabre, it's all in good fun and helps fund programs that are at risk, what with declining tax revenues. Maybe it's not to everyone's taste, but with a mailing list of over 30,000 people, I doubt that the department is losing a lot of sleep over that.

THE BOYS OF SUMMER

The Lefty

Sanford "Sandy" Koufax of the Brooklyn and subsequently Los Angeles Dodgers had a brief but illustrious career that was tragically cut short by severe arthritis. He was named the National League's Most Valuable Player in 1963 and won the Cy Young Award, which annually honors each league's best pitcher, in 1963, 1965 and 1966—each time by unanimous vote. In those three seasons, he led the league in the three major categories of earned run average, wins and strikeouts. He was the first major-league pitcher to throw more than three no-hitters. On September 9, 1965, Koufax became the sixth pitcher of the modern era of baseball (which began in 1900) to throw a perfect game (a perfect game is one in which a pitcher pitches a full nine innings in which no batter from the opposing team gets to first base). Because he retired so early, Koufax became the youngest player ever elected to the Baseball Hall of Fame; he was inducted just after his 36th birthday in 1972. On June 4 of that year, his number, 32, was retired in his honor.

DID YOU  **KNOW?**

Sandy Koufax was Jewish, and he refused to pitch Game 1 of the 1965 World Series because it fell on Yom Kippur, the Jewish Day of Atonement.

"Big D"

Don Drysdale, born in 1936 in Van Nuys, was a Dodgers team-mate of Koufax's, and together they formed one of the most for-midable pitching duos in baseball history. Drysdale intimidated batters with the brushback pitch, which forces a batter to move away from the plate out of fear that he will be hit, and the side-arm fastball, where the arm swings out parallel to the ground rather than overhand. Drysdale won the Cy Young Award for best pitcher in 1962, a year ahead of Sandy Koufax. In 1968, he set a record with 58 scoreless innings, a record not broken for 20 years. In fact, when Dodger Orel Hershiser was on the verge of breaking the record on September 28, 1988, he almost declined to pitch the 10th shutout inning out of respect for Drysdale, but Drysdale himself convinced him to try for the record. When Hershiser suc-ceeded, Drysdale went out to hug him and said "Oh, I'll tell ya, congratulations. And at least you kept it in the family."

Fernandomania

That would be Fernando Valenzuela that everyone was going crazy for in 1981, after the 20-year-old rookie for the Dodgers was called in to replace an injured player and pitched a shut-out on Opening Day, then went on to pitch eight winning games in a row. Fans from the Hispanic community of the region turned out in droves, and they weren't the only ones. Wherever the Dodgers went that year, they were sure of a huge attendance. Valenzuela became the only major league player in history to win the Rookie of the Year Award and the Cy Young Award in the same year.

Crossing the Line

Although born in Cairo, Georgia, in 1919, Baseball Hall of Fame honoree Jackie Robinson can still claim Southern California roots. His family moved to Pasadena in 1920. He went to both high school and junior college there, transferring to UCLA in 1939. Although Robinson is associated so strongly in our minds with baseball, while at UCLA, he actually lettered in *four* sports—baseball, football, basketball and track—and is still the only person to have done so. Of course, despite many subsequent awards in major league baseball, including the first ever Rookie of the Year Award and the Most Valuable Player Award of 1949, his enduring fame comes from his being the first African American to break the color line that segregated modern baseball. This historic moment took place on April 15, 1947, when he joined the Brooklyn Dodgers (later to become the Los Angeles Dodgers) in playing the Boston Braves as first baseman.

DID YOU KNOW?

All major league teams retired Robinson's number, 42, in recognition of his breaking of the color barrier.

Is There a Numerologist in the House?
A sad but historic moment for the Los Angeles Dodgers came on April 8, 1974, when Dodger pitcher Alphonso "Al" Downing pitched the ball that Hank Aaron hit for his 715th homerun, thereby breaking Babe Ruth's record.

Larger than Life Lasorda

No look at the Dodgers would be complete without at least
a passing mention of legendary Dodgers manager Tommy
Lasorda, who, in addition to leading the Dodgers to two National
League Championship wins and two World Series wins during
his 20 years in the role, was just possibly the team's number one
fan. He is famously quoted as having said, "I bleed Dodger blue,
and when I die, I'm going to the big Dodger in the sky."

Mr. Padre

Anthony "Tony" Gwynn spent his entire 20-year career with the
San Diego Padres. He was statistically one of the best and most
consistent hitters in baseball. He struck out only 434 times in
9288 career at-bats. He was elected to the Baseball Hall of Fame
on January 9, 2007, during his first year of eligibility, by 532
out of 545 ballots. He is the first National League member born
during the 1960s to be so honored.

So far, five other men who've played for the San Diego Padres
have become Hall of Famers: first baseman Willie McCovey,
pitcher Roland "Rollie" Fingers, pitcher Gaylord Perry, shortstop
Ozzie Smith and outfielder Dave Winfield. All of them have
had careers for other teams as well. So far, only Winfield has
chosen to be inducted as a Padre, although Tony Gwynn is certain to join him, since the Padres was his only team.

Angelic Players

Although the Los Angeles Angels of Anaheim have also claimed
Hall of Famers as teammates, none of them has been inducted
as an Angel. But a few have been significant enough in the
team's history to have their numbers retired in their honor:

☛ Jamaican-born batter Rod Carew, No. 29, was an American
League All-Star every year from 1967 to 1984.

☞ Pitcher Nolan Ryan, No. 30, was nicknamed "Ryan's Express" because of pitches that regularly reached 100 miles per hour. He still holds many pitching records, despite having retired in 1993—his 5714 career strikeouts, for example. He played for the Angels from 1972–79.

☞ Jimmy Reese, No. 50, began coaching the Angels in 1972 and remained active in the team's affairs until his death in 1994 at the age of 92. He must have been a pretty good coach, because Nolan Ryan named one of his sons Reese in his honor.

☞ Jim Fregosi, No. 11, a shortstop, managed the Angels from 1978–81 and in 1979 led them to the American League Western Division Championship, their first title in the 19 years of their existence.

DID YOU KNOW?

One other number has been retired by the Angels. It's number 26, which stands for the 26th man on the Angels' team—the original owner of the franchise, none other than the singing cowboy of early movie fame, Gene Autry.

Like Son, Like Father

A notable moment, though perhaps not a particularly happy one for California Angels fans, came on September 14, 1990, when Ken Griffey Jr. and his father Ken Griffey Sr. of the Seattle Mariners became the only father and son to hit back-to-back home runs in a major league baseball game.

FOR THE TALL AND TALL AT HEART

Two Time's the Charm

The Los Angeles Lakers have had not one but two great teams in recent years. The first included Kareem Abdul-Jabbar (born Ferdinand Lewis Alcindor) and Earvin "Magic" Johnson under the coaching of Pat Riley. In the 1980s, they appeared in the National Basketball Association (NBA) finals eight times, winning the championship five times, including consecutive wins in 1987 and 1988, the first time this had happened since the Boston Celtics won two in a row in 1968 and 1969.

Abdul-Jabbar is considered one of the best basketball players of all time. He is the all-time leading NBA scorer, with 38,387 points, and is certainly one of those with the most longevity. Playing 1560 games in 20 seasons, he is surpassed in the NBA only by Robert Parish, who played for 21 seasons. Abdul-Jabbar was known for his trademark "sky hook," a hook shot that he let go at the farthest extension of his outstretched hand, which, because he was over seven feet tall, was almost impossible to defend against.

In May 2006, ESPN rated Magic Johnson as the best point guard of all time. But he was also known for his ability to play all five positions well, especially in a pinch. He was one of the greatest ball-handlers and passers, and he was famous for his "no-look" passes, which confounded foes and teammates alike. He shocked the nation in 1991 with his announcement that he was HIV positive and was retiring from basketball, but came back to play on the All-Star team in 1992. He has in fact returned briefly to basketball several times since that decision.

Another Lakers winning streak came after Phil Jackson was hired to coach the team in 1999. With a strong team led by star athletes Shaquille O'Neal and Kobe Bryant, the Lakers won three consecutive NBA titles from 2000 to 2002. However, Bryant and O'Neal were in the news from 2001 on for a growing feud between them, which seemed to be fueled by their wins as much as their losses. O'Neal has since moved on to play for the Miami Heat, and in 2006, the two players shook hands and were even seen laughing together during the 2006 All-Star game.

THE OL' PIGSKIN

Something's Missing

When it comes to team sports, the L.A. region offers an embarrassment of riches. If you love baseball, you have the Dodgers and the Angels. If you're a basketball fan, you have the Lakers and the Clippers. Even professional hockey, which you might not immediately think of as a Southern California kind of sport, has two teams—the Anaheim Ducks and the Los Angeles Kings. And of course, the bitter rivalry between USC and UCLA ensures that there will be two collegiate teams to vie for your affections in practically every sport you can think of. But when it comes to pro football, you will look in vain, unless you look south to San Diego, where the Chargers currently have their home. It comes as something of a shock to realize that Los Angeles, one of the major cities of the United States, has not been able to keep a professional football team.

Los Angeles has had a pro football team in the past—three times, in fact. The NFL's Cleveland Rams came west in 1946, playing in Los Angeles for 34 seasons. In 1980, they moved to Anaheim, though they chose to keep the name of Los Angeles Rams. This left the L.A. venue open for the Oakland Raiders to come south, and they made it their home starting in 1982. But in the mid-1990s, both teams were offered more lucrative deals and modernized stadiums elsewhere—the Rams in St. Louis and the Raiders back in their original home, Oakland. So in 1995, the greater Los Angeles area went from having two pro teams to none. Although many interests would like to see this situation change, including Governor Arnold Schwarzenegger, the prohibitive costs of building a stadium in today's market, let alone coaxing a team to move there, remain challenging.

Another team that had an even briefer residence in Los Angeles was the AFL's Los Angeles Chargers. They began their life as a member of the newly formed American Football League in 1960 in Los Angeles, but within a year, they moved to San Diego, where they remain to the present day. The San Diego Chargers have been part of the NFL since the two leagues merged in 1970. The Chargers have so far had seven team members elected to the Pro Football Hall of Fame:

☞ wide receiver Lance Alworth, who, for his speed, grace, jumping ability and lithe build, was nicknamed "Bambi." He is considered by many to be the best wide receiver of the 1960s. He was the first San Diego Charger to be elected into the Hall of Fame.

☞ quarterback Dan Fouts, who led the Chargers to the play-offs every year from 1979 to 1982 and ended his career with over 40,000 passing yards—only the third player ever to do so.

☞ coach Sid Gillman, whose preference for deep downfield passes over the then more common short passes to running backs or receivers helped redefine the game.

☞ wide receiver Charles Joiner, who, while with the Chargers, exceeded 1000 yards received in a season for four seasons, and went to three Pro Bowls.

☞ David "Deacon" Jones, who was one of the greatest defensive ends of all time and was a Charger very briefly in 1972–73.

☞ Ron Mix, one of the original Los Angeles Chargers, who played guard and left tackle and was nicknamed the "Intellectual Assassin" because he somehow also found time to get a doctorate in law.

☞ tight end Kellen Winslow, who was not only able to make difficult catches but also had the speed to run the ball downfield.

Maybe They'll Have Better Luck Keeping *This* Kind of Football

Although soccer is a sport with growing appeal in the U.S., it has yet to become a national pastime in the way that, say, baseball is. But a little celebrity glamour never hurt any rising sport, and in January 2007, the major league soccer team known as the Los Angeles Galaxy discovered that it was shortly to be blessed with some. David Beckham, arguably the most recognizable athlete in the world, announced that he would be joining the Southern California club after his contract expired with the Spanish club Real Madrid in July.

GAME, SET, MATCH

A Lean, Mean, Tennis-Playing Machine

Born in Los Angeles in 1928 to a Mexican immigrant family, Ricardo "Pancho" Gonzales is considered one of the great tennis players of all time. He was completely self-taught. He dominated the world of men's tennis in the late 1950s and early '60s, winning the United States Professional Championship eight times and London's Wembly professional title four times. Because of the combination of his cannonball serve followed immediately by his vicious net game, there was a brief period in the '50s when the rules of tennis changed so that players had to wait for the ball to bounce once before returning the ball. But Gonzales continued to win anyway, so they changed the rule back.

Equal Pay for Equal Play

Billy Jean (Moffitt) King was born in Long Beach in 1943. She won a Southern California tournament at the age of 14 and played at Wimbledon in 1961, where she was defeated in singles but won in doubles with partner Karen Hantze Suzman. This was the first of a record 20 Wimbledon wins, including singles, doubles and mixed doubles. Her banner year was 1972, when she won the women's singles titles at Wimbledon, the U.S. Open and the French Open. She was named *Sport's Illustrated*'s "Sportsperson of the Year," being not only the first woman but also the first tennis player to receive the honor, and *Sports* magazine named her "Tennis Player of the Year." She was the first female athlete to win more than $100,000 in a single season, but this was still only one-third of what male tennis players made in prizes, which led her to successfully threaten a boycott of the U.S. Open unless women were fairly compensated.

"The Battle of the Sexes"

That really is what promoters called the much publicized tennis
match between Billy Jean King and retired tennis champion
Bobby Riggs that was held on September 20, 1973, at the
Houston Astrodome in Texas. At the height of the women's liberation movement, Riggs, another Los Angeles native, portrayed
himself as a male chauvinist who could easily take the best of
the current female tennis champions. He had already easily
beaten Margaret Court, then the top-ranked female tennis
player in the world. As he left the court in victory he said, "I
want Billy Jean King. I want the women's lib leader." King took
the challenge, for which she was paid $100,000 dollars. King
had learned Riggs' game from watching the match he played
against Court and ended up defeating him 6–4, 6–3, 6–3.
Whether Riggs, who was really a master showman and a self-
proclaimed tennis hustler, foresaw it or not, this nationally televised event did much to spark the American public's interest in
tennis, and women's tennis in particular. And despite all the
hoopla, he and King became and remained friends right up
until his death from prostate cancer in 1995.

SOME MORE SPECTACULAR SPORTS

No Place for Couch Potatoes

In Southern California, the mild weather means that many outdoor sports can be almost year-round activities. The region's mountain ranges provide hiking and biking opportunities galore, and even skiing during part of the year. The beachfront provides surfing at one of many world-renowned surf spots, long paths for rollerblading, walking or biking, and beach volleyball.

 Beach volleyball began in Santa Monica in the 1920s. Today, the Manhattan Beach Open, considered to be "the Wimbledon of beach volleyball," takes place right down the coast from Santa Monica. Its first tournament was in 1960.

A Day (or Three) at the Races

There are three famous horse racing tracks in Southern California:

☛ Santa Anita Race Track, a thoroughbred track, lies near the San Gabriel Mountains in Arcadia and is generally considered to offer the best wintertime horse racing in the U.S. and possibly even the world.

☛ Hollywood Park is located in Inglewood, not far from LAX. It opened in 1938, and its first chairman was Jack Warner of Warner Brothers fame, so not surprisingly, many of its first shareholders were Hollywood celebrities. Al Jolson once sat on the Board of Directors.

☛ And Los Alamitos offers some of the most lucrative stakes in the world in its specialty, Quarter Horse racing. It began offering year-round Quarter Horse racing in 2001.

The Sport of Kings

Speaking of horses, at Will Rogers State Historical Park, you can still watch a game of polo every weekend from April to November. Rogers, the famous American humorist, bequeathed his estate, including the polo fields, to the state of California in 1944 on the condition that it would continue to be used for polo and other equestrian purposes. Today, it is the only polo field in the Los Angeles area.

Xtremely Entertaining
Los Angeles' Staples Center is the current home of the summer X Games, a multi-sport event that usually takes place in August and focuses on extreme sports, including skateboarding, BMX bike competitions, an every-man-for-himself climbing event and wakeboarding. The first competition was called the Extreme Games and took place in Rhode Island and Vermont in 1995. It was renamed the X Games the following year.

Float Like a Predator

Tony Hawk is one of the preeminent figures in vertical skateboarding, also known as "vert," in which the skateboarder uses the steepness of an incline to become temporarily airborne. Hawk invented many skateboard tricks, but he is perhaps most famous for being the first to nail the "900" (two and a half rotations in the air, equaling 900 degrees, before landing again).

A FURY OF FIRSTS AND FAMOUS FEATS

☛ The Constitution of the State of California, California's first constitution, was drafted in Monterey in October 1849.

☛ According to the Borax company website, borates were discovered in California's Death Valley in 1881. This was the second such discovery in North America, the first being in Nevada in 1872.

☛ Los Angeles is home to the International Church of the Foursquare Gospel. Built in 1918, the temple was also the platform for messages delivered by Canadian-born Sister Aimee Semple McPherson—one of America's first female, and first famous, Pentecostal evangelists.

☛ Beverly Homer Delay, more commonly (and perhaps mercifully) known as B.H. Delay, was an early aviator and movie stunt pilot. In addition to many movie stunt firsts, he has a couple of Southern California firsts to his credit as well. His airfield, Delay Field, was the first lighted airport in the United States (1921), and he was responsible for the first aerial patrol in the nation (also 1921), which was ready to perform sea rescues, complete with flotation devices, at a moment's notice.

☛ California hotelier James Vail was the first in the world to coin the term "motel" by blending the words "motor hotel" together. He also opened the first such establishment on December 12, 1925, in San Luis Obispo, aptly naming it the Milestone Motel.

☛ California's first NASCAR race was held at the Carrell Speedway in Gardena on April 8, 1951.

☛ Edwards Air Force Base near Rosamond has its own world record to brag about. It was at this location where a Voyager aircraft, piloted by Richard Rutan and Jeana Yeager, took flight for the first-ever nonstop round-the-world trip. It left on December 14, 1986, and returned on December 23, clocking 216 hours and 25,000 miles in the process.

☛ Rosemead is home to Dave Moore. Who, you may ask? Back in 1989, Dave constructed the world's largest bicycle. The "Frankencycle" stood 11.1 feet in height with a front wheel diameter of 10 feet.

☛ Palos Verdes currently holds claim to being hometown of the youngest tennis player in history to win the U.S. Open men's title. Back in 1990, at just 19 years old, Pete Sampras won the tournament.

☛ Oxnard is home to the largest kosher winery on the West Coast. Herzog Wine Cellars opened their 77,000-square-foot facility in summer 2005.

☛ Six Flags Magic Mountain in Valencia currently boasts one of the world's fastest, tallest and longest roller coasters. "Tatsu" hits speeds of 62 miles per hour, and the track is 170 feet high and 3602 feet long. This most recent of the park's 17 record-setting rides opened for business in May 2006. Six Flags Magic Mountain, founded in 1961, is also the world's largest regional theme park company.

☛ As if you didn't already know, the world's largest movie studio is none other than Universal Studios Hollywood in Los Angeles.

☛ The Library Tower in Los Angeles is famous for two reasons. At a height of 1018 feet, it's considered the tallest building west of the Mississippi River, and it is the world's tallest building featuring a roof helipad.

☛ The city of Selma calls itself the "Raisin Capital of the World." It's hard to believe otherwise, because it claims to grow more than 90 percent of the world's raisins within a 40-mile radius. Hmmm.

☛ A 1700-pound camel named Bert is considered the world's highest ranking law-enforcement camel. The dromedary was sworn in for duty with the Los Angeles County Sheriff's Department in San Dimas on April 5, 2003. Admittedly, his role is more a public relations one than a crime fighting one.

☛ Fallbrook calls itself the "Avocado Capital of the World."

☛ The rural community of Baker, with a population of just over 900, must simply attract modern-day gold seekers. Maybe it's because visitors and other passing traffic often stop there, but the country store in that community claims to have sold more winning California State Lottery tickets than any other outlet in the state.

THE 10 BEST REASONS TO LIVE IN SOUTHERN CALIFORNIA

1. Okay, just to start us off, how could anyone not want to live in a state with an official fossil called *Smilodon californicus*? And how much better is it that this turns out to be a saber-toothed cat?

2. Don't even get me started on the tar pits. (Actually, asphalt pits, but who's checking?) How cool is it that you can walk right up to a stinking, bubbling ooze and know that just under the surface lie remnants of the primordial past, just waiting to be pulled out? Believe me, that fake movie *Volcano*, in which Wilshire Boulevard gets inundated with a molten river of lava (no way), has nothing on this little bit of reality.

3. You could be sitting in your local Starbucks and your favorite movie star might just walk in and order a cappuccino. Or you might be going to your dentist appointment and there he is, getting into the elevator ahead of you. Or she's on location with a film crew shooting *just down the street* from where you work. I know, I know—that's, like, *three* good reasons to live in Southern California. Of course, it could also be your least favorite movie star, and he could be obnoxious, but that's the risk you take.

4. Where else can you rent out your house to a Hollywood production company for a week and have enough to live on for several months thereafter?

5. Let's see—beach or snow? Snow or beach? With easy access to both, these are the kind of taxing questions that Southern Californians are forced to occupy themselves with *all the time.*

6. Public art, people. Everywhere you look, there's another freaking mural.

7. Call it envy if you want, but let's face it, the rest of Americans, especially Northern Californians, pretty much hate Southern Californians. But being one, you not only won't care, you won't even notice.

8. There are a lot of people here, from every imaginable corner of the globe, increasing your chances of meeting someone interesting. True, there's a downside—i.e., there are a *lot* of people here, and a good percentage of them are probably richer, better looking, more intelligent and more talented than you are. Sorry.

9. Cheer up. Southern California reinvents itself constantly. You can too.

10. There really *is* just something about the light.

ABOUT THE AUTHORS

Seana Graham

Seana Graham was born in Santa Monica and grew up in Venice Beach and Buena Park. As a child, she loved her family's visits to Knott's Berry Farm, especially the dubious thrill of being robbed by a bandit on horseback during the stagecoach ride. Her family later moved to the Bay Area and then to Denver, Colorado, but the L.A. area is in Seana's blood. These days, she makes her home in Santa Cruz, where she attended college. She now works as a bookseller and buyer for a locally owned bookstore, and her short stories have appeared in numerous magazines, literary journals, and anthologies.

Lisa Wojna

Lisa Wojna, author of several nonfiction books, has worked in the community newspaper industry as a writer and journalist and has traveled all over Canada, from the windy prairies of Manitoba to northern British Columbia, and even to the wilds of Africa. Although writing and photography have been a central part of her life for as long as she can remember, it's the people behind every story that are her motivation and give her the most fulfillment.

ABOUT THE ILLUSTRATORS

Peter Tyler

Peter is a recent graduate of the Vancouver Film School visual art and design and classical animation programs. Although his ultimate passion is for filmmaking, he is also intent on developing his draftsmanship and storytelling, with the aim of using those skills in future filmic misadventures.

Roger Garcia

Roger Garcia immigrated to Canada from El Salvador at the age of seven. Because of the language barrier, he had to find a way to communicate with other kids. That's when he discovered the art of tracing. It wasn't long before he mastered this highly skilled technique, and by age 14 he was drawing weekly cartoons for the *Edmonton Examiner*. He taught himself to paint and sculpt, and then in high school and college, Roger skipped class to hide in the art room all day in order to further explore his talent. Currently, Roger's work can be seen in a local weekly newspaper and in places around Edmonton, Alberta.